ESCAPE TO Northern New England

Photography by Peter Guttman
Text by Patricia Harris *&* David Lyon

Fodor's

FODOR'S TRAVEL PUBLICATIONS
NEW YORK • TORONTO • LONDON • SYDNEY • AUCKLAND • WWW.FODORS.COM

Escape to Northern New England

COPYRIGHT © 2003 BY FODORS LLC

Photographs copyright © 2002 by Peter Guttman

Fodor's is a registered trademark of Random House, Inc.

All rights reserved under International and Pan-American Copyright Conventions. Published in the United States by Fodor's Travel Publications, a unit of Fodors LLC, a subsidiary of Random House, Inc., and simultaneously in Canada by Random House of Canada Limited, Toronto. Distributed by Random House, Inc., New York.

No illustrations or other portions of this book may be reproduced in any form without written permission from the publisher.

While every care has been taken to ensure the accuracy of the information in this guide, time brings change, and consequently, the publisher cannot accept responsibility for errors that may occur. Call ahead to verify prices and other information.

First Edition

ISBN 1-4000-1202-3

Special Sales

Fodor's Travel Publications are available at special discounts for bulk purchases for sales promotions or premiums. Special editions, including personalized covers, excerpts of existing guides, and corporate imprints, can be created in large quantities for special needs. For more information, contact your local bookseller or write to Special Markets, Fodor's Travel Publications, 280 Park Ave., New York, NY 10017. Inquiries from Canada should be directed to your local Canadian bookseller or sent to Random House of Canada, Ltd., Marketing Dept., 2775 Matheson Boulevard East, Mississauga, Ontario L4W 4P7. Inquiries from the United Kingdom should be sent to Fodor's Travel Publications, 20 Vauxhall Bridge Road, London, England SW1V 2SA.

PRINTED IN GERMANY

10 9 8 7 6 5 4 3 2 1

Library of Congress Cataloging-in-Publication Data available upon request.

Acknowledgments

Peter Guttman blissfully sampled New England's abundance of lobster pounds and sugar shacks during his grueling research. With gratitude for life's many blessings, kudos to David Lyon and Patricia Harris for palpably sensuous writing. Travel companions enduring myriad visual experiments and considerably shortening Interstate 91 receive warmest appreciation: caring friends Bruce and Peggy Hart, magnificent support from Jennifer Hawkins, spontaneous efforts of Lynn Bernstein, and as always, dazzling inspiration of Lori Greene and Chase Guttman. Finally, big thanks for the artistic wisdom of Fabrizio La Rocca and Tigist Getachew who synthesized a ballet from a thousand steps.

From Patricia Harris and David Lyon: Thanks to Julia Dillon for the good word, to Peter Guttman for showing us new angles on what we thought we already knew, to Laura Kidder for gently insisting on just the right words, and to Fabrizio La Rocca for developing a series that's as much fun to write as to read. Special thanks to Paul Kendall and his horses, to Ed Mathieu and his dogs, and to innkeepers who eased our journeys. Thank you, Rick and Karen Miles, for keeping the flame alive. David tips a plaid cap to trapper John Guptill, who long ago taught him just how wild the woods can be.

Credits

Creative Director and Series Editor: Fabrizio La Rocca

Editorial Director: Karen Cure

Art Director: Tigist Getachew

Editor: Laura Kidder

Editorial Assistant: Dennis Sarlo

Production Editor: Kristin Milavec

Production/Manufacturing: C. R. Bloodgood, Robert B. Shields

Maps: David Lindroth, Inc.

Other Escape Guides

Escape to the Amalfi Coast • Escape to the American Desert
Escape to the Wine Country • Escape to Ireland
Escape to Morocco • Escape to New Zealand • Escape to
Provence • Escape to the Riviera • Escape to Tuscany
Available in bookstores

Most books on the travel shelves are either long on the nitty-gritty and short on evocative photographs, or the other way around. We at Fodor's think the balance in this slim volume is just perfect, rather like the intersection of the most luscious magazine article and a sensible, down-to-earth guidebook. On the road, the useful pages at the end of the book are practically all you need. For the planning, roam through the stories and the photographs up front: each reveals a key facet of the vast and variegated country of northern New England, and conveys a sense of place that will take you there before you go. Each page opens up to exceptional experiences; each spread leads you to the region's spirit at its purest.

Some of these places are sure to beckon. You may yearn to wipe the salt spray from your brow as you reef the sails of a wooden ship. You may long to feel your neck muscles twitch with the snap of a perfect cast as you deposit a gossamer fly onto a wilderness stream. You may imagine lolling on a sandy shore, book folded on your lap, as strains of Mozart float from the woods. You may crave the sting of alpine air on your cheeks as you skate-ski through a forest, bound for a warm toddy by the fire. Plant yourself on a tumble-down stone wall

and open a slim volume to Robert Frost's country wisdom. Fall in with the townsfolk as they march to their fairgrounds on the Fourth of July. Paint your face and howl at the moon for Halloween.

To capture the essence of northern New England, authors Patricia Harris and David Lyon and photographer Peter Guttman hiked the ridges of the Green Mountains and mushed across the frozen wastes of northern Maine. They cracked lobster with smooth stones, graded vials of maple syrup, and even took knife and fork to helpings of stewed beaver. In their journeys they shivered at the midnight call of loons, contemplated the silence of Shaker haunts, and learned to distinguish a horse's walk from its formal trot. And never once, they agree, did they encounter the fabled Yankee reserve. Some myths, it seems, are groundless.

Generations of travelers before them have experienced the power and magic of the region firsthand, and so will you. Forget your projects and deadlines, and escape to northern New England. You owe it to yourself.

—The Editors

AS THE MAIL BOAT COURSES THROUGH LOBSTER BUOYS AND ROUNDS Robinson Point, you spy the stubby light that beckons storm-lashed fishermen to safety on the leeward side of Isle au Haut. You'll sleep tonight beneath that light in the Keeper's House—a refuge from the raging world. Although a few small dwellings huddle near Town Landing, half the island belongs to Acadia National Park, with its rugged spruce forest, towering bluffs, and shores of slate and granite ledge. It's midsummer, and there's not a tour bus anywhere, you note with glee, setting off on foot along the only road. On the headland above Moores Harbor, you recall Thoreau: "In wildness is the preservation of the world." Black-backed gulls dance only feet away on updrafts off the cliff. You're determined now to reach the water and half run

To the Lighthouse

ISLE AU HAUT, DOWN EAST MAINE

The 48-foot-tall Isle au Haut lighthouse—only half the height of most Maine beacons—has summoned sailors home since Christmas Eve 1907.

as you follow blue blazes through the woods to emerge, at last, at Eben's Head. Rollers clatter rounded rocks like castanets, and you clamber onto the ledges, following the archaic cairns that others left as markers. Reaching a stony point, you recline on sun-hot rock, surrounded by the primal crash of breaking waves. When a sharp whiff of ozone signals the wind shift—the wind never stops, only changes direction—your body knows it's time to seek shelter. You rush down the long dirt drive to the Keeper's House and a feast of phyllo-wrapped lobster by the soft glow of an oil-lamp chandelier. When gloaming fades to dark, you mount the point, straining to behold other beacons conversing across the straits from Saddleback, Vinalhaven, and—faint as a distant star—Matinicus. When you finally bed down in the Keeper's Room, you decipher the light's slow, steady wink, as reassuring as a heart beat. "Home safe," it seems to say.

From spruce-hooded trails to the crusted rocks of its shore, Isle au Haut is ideal for perfecting the art of doing nothing. In time, you get quite good at it.

I thought as I lay there, half awake and half asleep, looking upward through the window at the lights above my head, how many sleepless eyes from far out on the Ocean stream—mariners of all nations spinning their yarns through the various watches of the night—were directed toward my couch.

—Henry David Thoreau, "Highland Light"
(from Cape Cod, *1865)*

THE LANKY TEEN IN THE PLAID FLANNEL SHIRT WAVES BOTH ARMS LIKE a big-city traffic cop and yells, "The tall trees are way back on the ridge." He pivots and waves his arms the other way: "The real full ones are down in the hollow." The Rocks estate bristles with balsams dusted with the confectioners' sugar of overnight snow. Parents and kids hop down from a horse-drawn wagon, pick up bucksaws, and begin the quest for a perfect Christmas tree. Snow crunches and squeaks underfoot. A father stands next to a broad specimen—about 6 feet, measured by the top of his head. "Too short," his daughter pronounces, her cheeks rouged from the cold. His son spots a taller, more conical candidate. Dad can barely reach the top of it with his fingertips. "Just right," his young arbiter declares. Back at the barn, wreaths are stacked next to

North Country Christmas

BETHLEHEM AND STARK, NEW HAMPSHIRE

The first snowfall transforms the landscape into a blank slate of possibility, making everyone feel a little younger.

trees that wait to be baled. North country crafters arrange their wares—ornaments, chutneys, hand-knit mittens, embroidered aprons. This holiday needs neither malls nor Muzak. You climb into the shelter of your car and can't help humming "O Little Town of Bethlehem" on the drive into the village with its one-road center of galleries, antiques shops, and a general store. At the Bethlehem Methodist Church fair's bake table you fill a decorated coffee can with homemade cookies, provender for the back-roads journey north. As you round the bend on Route 10, Stark jumps out of the early dusk. Lights twinkle on its covered bridge, on the Union Church belfry, and on the tree that marks the turn. Across the Ammonoosuc River, electric candles glow in the windows of the Stark Village Inn. The scent of wood smoke wafts through the silent night, and you know that the innkeeper has laid a crackling fire in the hearth.

From daytime forays into the winter landscape
to the warm pleasures of home and hearth,
Christmas unfolds in a series of ceremonies that
recapture the wonder of a child.

YOU SEIZE THE STEERING WHEEL AT 10 O'CLOCK AND 2, ALL THE BETTER to take the curves, and poise your left foot over the clutch, ready to downshift if—or when—a moose lurches onto the road. Cracked and heaved from frosts of winters past, the asphalt ribbon of the "Kanc" twists 34 miles through the White Mountain National Forest. The road, though, is its own destination. You punch the gas and burst into the hardwood brilliance, tunneling through acid-yellow birches and beeches, buzzing past incendiary red and orange maples, blasting through a bronze cascade of leaves loosed by an army of oaks. Priapic stands of staghorn sumac leer, crimson with yearning. On the western approach, the roadbed rises and falls with the rough convulsions of mountain valleys scratched out by glaciers. You downshift to mount

Drivers Wanted

FOLIAGE SEASON ON NEW HAMPSHIRE'S KANCAMAGUS HIGHWAY

Look back and wonder about the home state of the car behind you. In autumn, the Kanc attracts drivers from across North America.

2,000 feet in the first 10 miles, then pop over Kancamagus Pass, where the Swift River flows east to the Saco, and the Pemigewasset flows back west to the sea. A flick of the wrist slips the car into fifth gear to freewheel down a seven-degree incline, where even dawdlers accelerate. In this snaking descent, the windshield fills with road and trees at once. When the Kanc straightens and flattens, you pull over at the boulder-strewn pawtucket of Lower Falls. The forest is pungent with the tannic bite of dead leaves, the acrid snap of dry mosses. The shallows of the Swift River chatter over rocks and swirl near the bank in cold, green eddies. Electric in the falling angle of light, Norway maples are hung with a scarlet halo, intermediary between sky and earth. A leaf lets go from its branch and descends, rocking on the wind, into the water's froth. It skitters downstream and finally vanishes.

A single leaf can be as beautiful as an entire landscape. Find a still point to stop, and step to the edge of the silent woods.

ONE HUNDRED YEARS OF SNOWS HAVE FALLEN SINCE THE LAST GRAND hotel rose in the White Mountains. Like a great white ark beached among the peaks, the Mount Washington Hotel & Resort stands in a veil of softly falling flurries. It exemplifies the Gilded Age philosophy that you don't have to rough it in the wilderness. Bellhops in down vests stash bags for guests who are eager to skate-ski Upper Honeymoon, hop herringbones to higher ground, speed down the wooded length of the Tim Nash Trail— leaping each small brook and minimogul—before returning to the hotel via an abandoned rail bed. A swift run leaves time for a martini in the Conservatory before dressing for dinner. (Gentlemen: jackets, please.) The band strikes up a tune as diners sashay to their assigned tables. After dessert, it's time for a few turns on the dance

Dress Whites

WINTER AT NEW HAMPSHIRE'S GRAND MOUNTAIN RESORTS

In northern New Hampshire, it can be hard to see where the White Mountains end and the rest of the Appalachian chain begins.

floor; the tenor sax solo on "Unforgettable" brings a round of applause. Farther north, the Balsams Grand Resort Hotel revels in the deep snows of Dixville Notch. Instead of a run on the alpine slope, you can opt for snowshoes—with crampons fore and aft— and make the sharp ascent to Table Rock, set high against an often royal-blue sky. The English language should have more words for "white" and a name for the way snow smells in high-altitude sunlight. Québec is to the northwest, the Rangeley Peaks to the northeast. Beneath Abenaki Mountain, the Balsams cuts a fairy-tale figure of peaked gables. The hush of late afternoon settles in throughout the hotel like an intake of breath before a great sigh. Lamps wink on. Waiters move crisply about the dining room, carefully creasing white linens and arranging crystal and silver. There is, after all, a proper way to take the measure of the wilds.

The Mount Washington Hotel & Resort takes
its name from the mountain that looms behind
it. Like the leader for whom it was named,
this tallest peak in the Presidential Range
is first among equals.

Among the few survivors from a gracious era
of stately lodgings, the sprawling Balsams
Grand Resort Hotel represents a warm refuge
in scenic but rugged terrain.

COUPLES ARE BOUND TO FEEL NAUGHTY MOUNTING ONE OF THE TWO staircases to the light-filled guest rooms in Enfield's Great Stone Dwelling. In the Shaker days, women entered on the east, men on the west. Reverence still clings to the rooms where the brothers and sisters led their private lives: separate, equal, intimate only with God. You hang your jacket on one of the wooden pegs that line the walls, fold your clothes away neatly, and flush as you eye the queen-size bed. The lyrics of a Shaker song—"Tis a gift to be simple"—ring true amid the dwelling's 500 built-in cupboards, 800 drawers, and countless peg hooks. Halfway across the state the Canterbury Shaker community rolls down gracefully from its hilltop. Its buildings seem only momentarily vacant, as if everyone has just stepped out to do chores. You stride

Peace on Earth

SHAKER COMMUNITIES IN ENFIELD & CANTERBURY, NEW HAMPSHIRE

The Shaker way of living epitomizes the still life, radiant with the inherent godliness of unadorned simplicity.

through an arbor of sugar maples to the 1792 meetinghouse, where men entered on the left, women on the right. Dark pegs in the floor dictate precisely where brothers and sisters could stand for the worshipful dance—just so close, and no closer. In the Creamery Restaurant you order a hearty traditional meal: dill bread and smoked pork chops smothered in maple barbecue sauce. The sect's legacy lives on in so many ways—flat brooms, nesting oval boxes, straight-back chairs devoid of ornament. The whine of lathes and *tack-tack-tack* of small hammers emanate from the workshop as museum craftsmen turn spindles for a chair and assemble the dovetail joints of a box. Transfixed in the pious silence of the laundry—where a soapy scent still lingers—you gaze out to the fields and expect to see the brethren appear from below the rise, striding in time to a hymn with 10-foot-long trays on their collective shoulders, casting seed upon the fecund earth.

No Shaker believer has inhabited Canterbury Shaker Village for more than a decade, but the sect's ways of work and worship are well preserved in the museum.

The Great Stone Dwelling at
Enfield, once the largest building
between Boston and Montréal,
allows guests of the Shaker Inn
to abide for a while amid
craftsmanship that embodies the
Shaker philosophy and spirit.

PITY THE POOR MAPMAKER. MAINE'S SHATTERED COAST TWISTS AND darts 2,500 miles. Peninsulas and islands dangle off the mainland like a fisherman's baited lines. Every convolution of the baroque shoreline between Portland and Rockland hides a cove, every cove an anchorage, and every anchorage a lobster boat with a tall pilot house and low, flat gunwales. The rude diesels roar as the lobstermen steam from buoy to buoy, hauling lines on the power winch, lifting the metal-mesh traps aboard to empty and bait them, then returning them to the ocean floor. *Homarus americanus* is their quarry. The mottled green-and-bronze crustaceans flap and flail as they exit the numbing brine. To taste your own, follow the roads that snake down from Old Route 1 through salt marsh and forest, passing placid duck ponds and rushing

Tail and Claw

LOBSTER HARBORS OF THE MAINE PENINSULAS

Lobstermen head out to sea to haul their traps daily because captive lobsters turn on each other, and only the largest survives.

freshets. No-nonsense concrete bridges squat above the narrows that cleave island from the main. Along the way, fishermen's cottages hunker low, their dooryards facing a southerly sun. The twisting route resolves abruptly at the village harbor, dotted with tenders and distant wooded islets. The hard blue light is dazzling. The town dock bobs in a stew of aromas: the faint but clinging stink of bait, the fresh scent of kelp, the snuff of wooden planks too long out in the weather. Every piling is crowned with mendicant gulls whose rusty squawks fade in the wind. A lobsterman unloads his catch at the clapboard shack, where the agent, in turn, empties it into holding tanks out back. Inside, steam rises from kettles behind the counter. Five minutes after placing an order, a scarlet lobster—side of slaw, ear of corn—appears. Settled at a picnic table, you raise a rock to crack the shell and feast.

Lobster tastes best when freshly caught. And no place serves fresher lobster than the harborside shacks: the crustaceans often go from the bracing brine into boiling pots within minutes.

AS THE LAMP HISSES AND POPS INTO DARKNESS, THE STARS WINK ON, one by one, filling the bowl of Skylight Pond with pinpoints of light. Bone-weary, you slide into your bedroll and instantly fall asleep. Minutes later—or so it seems—dawn explodes over the distant peak of Mt. Moosilauke, filling the shelter with fiery light. The cloud of your breath hovers in the morning cold as you pull on your boots and shoulder your pack. The world has narrowed to what you can reasonably lug. The trail guide, the compass, and the tea bags made the list; the espresso pot did not. You fall into an easy rhythm on the trail, breaking stride only to negotiate a tangle of roots or step tentatively on dry stones to cross a stream. The granddaddy of American hiking paths undulates up Vermont's knobby backbone through a spruce

Not Just a Walk in the Woods

HIKING FROM HUT TO HUT ON VERMONT'S LONG TRAIL

To hike the Long Trail is to be initiated into the secret heart of Vermont, as intimate as a single tree, as vast as a forested mountain.

and hemlock forest where each step is muffled by brown pine needles in earthy decay. Finches twitter from the branches and squirrels rustle in the underbrush. Grunting up a narrow mountainside cut, you mutter for the umpteenth time, "No wonder they call it the *Long* Trail," and taste the copper bite of an adrenaline surge. Days later, under a blue sky, you march across Mt. Mansfield's wind-scoured tundra, where sedges and lichens cling to rock. You left pride behind miles ago, so there's no shame in practically sliding down the Adam's Apple before stumbling along a narrow trail to Taft Lodge. How many hikers will share this log shelter? What tales will they tell? When the time comes, you won't mention that tumble on Camel's Hump or that blister on your left heel. Instead, you'll speak of the moon rising over some distant range, of a fox teaching her kits to hunt, or of a morning rainbow arching above Lake Champlain.

Weather on the Long Trail can be volatile.
A single, subtle shift of the wind can
convert the evanescent warmth of Indian
summer into the biting snap of early winter.

How Sweet It Is

MAPLE FESTIVAL, WHITINGHAM, VERMONT

EVERY SUGAR MAKER IN WHITINGHAM KNOWS THAT ROUND ABOUT THE TIME OF TOWN MEETING—the first Tuesday in March—the tomato seeds are germinating in a south window, and the early sap is trickling. By maple festival weekend, it's really *plink-plink-plinking* down taps and into galvanized buckets hung on trees in the sugar bush for miles around. The whole town smells like a country breakfast: pungent wood smoke and a hint of maple. The Lions Club is flipping flapjacks to start the day. "I like a little pancake with my syrup," says a tall man with silver temples, urging the server to ladle on more of the liquid gold. Maple weekend is hardly a time for restraint, you agree, studying a map to the sugarhouses. Steve Morse's small red shack is deep in the woods. Jess and Molly, his black mares, haul the collecting sleigh over terrain too steep for a tractor. With the thermometer reading 40 by day, 20 by night, the sap is running strong. At Sprague's, thrifty Yankees have

It takes 40 gallons of sap laboriously collected from taps on the trees to produce a single gallon of glorious maple syrup.

transformed a church building once used by Carthusian monks into a sugarhouse. As steam billows off the evaporator, Karen Sprague offers samples of her maple candy and the maple cream that she's churned from extra-thick syrup. Over at Corse Farm, a hand-scrawled record on a wall shows the yields for every year since 1918. The Corses raise dairy cattle, too, and it's hard to refuse their offer of a maple milkshake. At day's end, the Masons put on a supper of ham, beans, and a curious dessert: boiled syrup drizzled over a bowl of snow. You peel off the cold, chewy stuff with a fork and savor its gummy maple intensity, then take back your bowl of snow for another hit. They call this taste of Vermont "sugar on snow."

OF COURSE IT'S COLD. THE NORTHWEST WIND IS WHISTLING OVER Mt. Kineo, sweeping into Lily Bay, and kicking granular crystals onto the fringes of Sugar Island. Harnessed to sleds that are tied to separate saplings, two dog teams eagerly paw the snowy ground. With each frigid gust, Indy and Klondike flatten their ears, squint their eyes, and raise their muzzles to bay with abandon. Their red-tinged fur riffles in the breeze. You tromp on the brake of your sled while head musher Ed Mathieu unfastens the ropes and takes his spot up ahead. "Rebel!" he calls to the lead dog. "Hike, hike!" His team of four huskies bolts down a trail, and his sled snaps into motion behind. "Hike, hike!" you say gently, knowing the dogs need little prodding. Silent as wolves, they set off and quickly find their rhythm. On the

Going to the Dogs

DOGSLEDDING AT MOOSEHEAD LAKE, MAINE

Blood rushes through your veins, and the wind takes your breath away as the huskies hurtle through the dark forest.

steepest hills you step off the runners and trot alongside the team before hopping back on and crouching to speed down the slopes. The clattering sled sends snow and ice flying on the turns. The winter air stings, and the hemlocks pass in a black and green blur. It's easy to imagine running with the pack. At midday Ed stops and produces a portable "sunflower" stove. Steam and the comforting aroma of chicken and rice rise from the pan. Toggled to a steel line, the dogs all rest on the snowpack—tucking their noses into their tails—all, that is, except Bud, a young mastiff-huskie mix that's chafing to run. Fortified by the meal, so are you. Later, back in the comfort of the Lodge at Moosehead Lake, you curl up beneath a canopy of moose antlers and dream of the dark forest, of bristled fur and hot breath, and of running, running, running without end.

The largest lake within a single state's borders, Moosehead is a gateway to Maine's North Woods. Winter ice can be treacherous, developing thin spots, but fishermen brave the frozen cap to seek elusive trout.

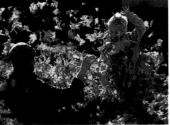

THE TOWN HAS A WORLD RECORD TO UPHOLD TODAY, AND legions of celebrants are lending their aid: families from 5 miles down the road, their neighbors from 50 miles around, their cousins from 500 miles away. Sticky to the elbows after scooping out seeds and strings, they're all giddy with the histrionics of Halloween. Like a phalanx of Druids, everyone shuffles in line with their globular offerings to the towers that rise like pagan altars honoring a harvest goddess. A five-year-old hugs a pumpkin with a gap-toothed grin as big as her own. Rural New Hampshire has reaped the final bounty from its orchards and fields. Ears of Indian corn hang by their husks to dry and jumbled baskets overflow with heirloom apples, dimpled squashes, and knobby gourds. Pyramids stacked with thousands of jack-o'-lanterns beg the question: is there a pumpkin in

City of Lights

PUMPKIN FESTIVAL, KEENE, NEW HAMPSHIRE

As the ripening season ends in a rush of color, every man, woman, and child is an artist, unleashing every pumpkin's hidden mask.

Monadnock country that hasn't yet gone under the knife? October is hastening to an end. The wind whispers of a coming cold, and the metallic scent of late-season rain rides the air. But the crowd has come to defy the elements, to frighten off the long darkness of winter by mocking the creatures of the night. Dracula readjusts his fangs. Wolfman scratches an itch on his furry hands. Witches and hobgoblins race and chase each other up and down the street, shouting "boo!" at pirates and ghosts. As dusk descends, the volunteer lighters move from pumpkin to pumpkin, igniting candles that, in turn, fill the streets with an orange glow. Like one great beast, the crowd lurches between light and shadow, throbbing to the beat of "The Monster Mash." The little ones chime in on the refrain of "Werewolves of London," howling "ow-ooh!" The grown-ups throw their heads back, cackle madly, lift their chins, and bay at the moon.

Great walls of jack-o'-lanterns blaze against the dark to celebrate Keene's harvest season. More than 23,000 carved pumpkins are offered up each year to secure the city's mark in the *Guinness Book of World Records*.

"WE'LL FOLLOW THE WIND," CAPTAIN RICK MILES EXPLAINS, GRINNING through his beard as the *Timberwind* clears Rockport's crowded harbor. Out in open water, he gives the order to hoist sail. The old salts untie the halyards—already even novices have learned to call them lines, not ropes—and all hands grab hold. The first mate sings the verse and everyone tugs between lines of the chorus. *Heave away! [Ummmpph.] Haul away! [Ummmpph.] We're bound for South Australia!* The canvas snaps to in the breeze. Prevailing westerlies send the schooner running Down East through the islands, seaward of Vinalhaven on a beeline toward Matinicus. Time and tide dictate shipboard life. You wake with coffee on deck to a glassy sea and a pink-and-purple dawn. The scent of brine is all around. A soft *plup* signals a porpoise

Heave Ho, Me Hearties

ABOARD THE SCHOONER *TIMBERWIND* ON MAINE'S PENOBSCOT BAY

The *Timberwind* harks back to an age of iron men and wooden ships. "She was built heavy and solid and tough," says Rick Miles.

surfacing. When a breeze rises, you crank the windlass to raise anchor as your shipmates hoist sail. Later you take the wheel to ease the 85-ton vessel past rocky islands tufted with spruce and fir. Ospreys and eagles circle overhead, then swoop and snatch a meal from the silver flash of schooling mackerel. Seals bark to salute the ship's passing, and, for the sheer joy of it, you bark back. Dark as tar, a cormorant unfolds its wings on a rock to dry them in the sun. The bell summons all hands below to Karen Miles's New England boiled dinner and deep-dish apple pie. You justify seconds by vowing to row the tender tomorrow to ferry the others ashore. On deck, the inky sky is awash with stars. Flashes warn of treacherous shoals, safely far away. Awed and comforted, you plunge back into the warm galley for a game of cribbage. Lulled by the scents of woolen sweaters and wood smoke, you clamber into your berth and sail to sleep.

Passengers and crew work hard—from
the galley's hot belly to the heights of the
masts—while cruising the island-dotted
waters of Penobscot Bay.

At sundown the wind subsides,
and the ship at anchor rocks
softly in the lapping waves.
The arc of darkness marches
east to west across the sky,
and lanterns glow on deck.

THE SCENTS OF RIPENED STRAW AND FRESH MANURE MINGLE IN THE warm air of the barn. At your footfall, the saddle horses—Dolly, Buffy, Suzy, and Sam—crane their necks expectantly, looking for water and oats. The big Belgian draft horses, Geo and Nick, snicker and shift in their stalls. Mama, the tortoiseshell cat, rubs your legs, then dashes underfoot as you continue past the barn to the gardens, stooping to bruise the fragrant leaves of lavender and lemon thyme. Mama grabs a stalk of catmint in her teeth and chews. You pilfer pea pods from the vines and crunch down—they're sugar-snap for sure. The Sweet 100 cherry tomatoes are beginning to set fruit, and already the kitchen staff has thinned the rows of spinach for salads and soufflés. Distracted by squabbling turkeys, Mama crouches, her tail switching back

King of the Hill

MOUNTAIN VIEW FARM, EAST BURKE, NORTHEAST KINGDOM, VERMONT

The mountaintop realm basks in the long light of a summer day, each blade of grass glimmering until the cows come home.

and forth. You leave her to her huntress games, gather up your blanket and picnic hamper, and follow the wagon path through a stand of hardwoods. Insistent as toddlers, bullet-headed mushrooms poke through remnants of last autumn's leaves. Maidenhair ferns loosen their grip on spring and welcome summer with open hands. Maybe tomorrow you'll scramble up and down narrow trails on a mountain bike, but for now you're satisfied to leave the glade for the crest of a high meadow. Across the hillside, cattle low. Timothy grass shines electric green, dotted with blooming clover. The first haying is only a week away, but that's someone else's worry. You unfurl the blanket, dig into the hamper, and uncork a bottle of Viognier. To the east—far beyond the cleft of a long, deep valley—the White Mountains carve a serrated horizon. Resting on your elbows, chin in both hands, you survey your Northeast Kingdom, close your eyes, and smile.

Surrounded by a courtyard of classic red barns, the Inn at Mountain View Farm stands sentinel amid an expanse of green fields. The inn's 440 acres form the core of a gentleman farmer's model estate established in 1883.

FAT SPATTERS ON THE BARBECUE GRILL AS A WIRY MAN WITH A bristly mustache eases his spatula under the moose patties and gives each an expert flip. "Out here, we'll do the moose and boar and maybe some venison steak," he says. "Be sure to try the *smoked* boar. It has the most flavor." The Congregational church's wild game supper, a tradition since 1956, is about to begin. "Nobody goes away hungry," says a church member in a blue blazer. It's hard to tell whether that's an observation or a command. "Start with the rabbit pie," advises an experienced diner. "It tastes just like chicken." Her friend demurs, praising the venison chili. They both tote Tupperware (for leftovers) in string bags. Upstairs, in the sanctuary, Harvey Bartlett—the church's deer-hunting, buffalo-jerky-making minister—folds his hands to his breast, scrunches

Please Pass the Pheasant Pâté

WILD GAME CHURCH SUPPER IN BRADFORD, VERMONT

The game supper is a homecoming. One congregant says that even visitors from afar "like to think of this as their little church."

his eyes shut, and beseeches heaven's blessings. His "amen" is a signal to rush the stairs, where the aroma of roasted meat rises from the hall below. In the buffet line, five guys in a row wear camouflage and Day-Glo–orange hats. They've been up since dawn, and not one has gotten a clear shot all day. "Game supper's a sure thing," the nearest hunter says, grinning and holding out his plate for extra helpings. The rabbit does remind you of chicken, and the chili is respectably hot. Beaver, you've been warned, is an acquired taste, and you try it gingerly. "Almost taste the bark they've been eating, eh?" the gent across the table asks with a chortle. But you're a sport, and clean your plate in time for gingerbread with real whipped cream. When you push back your chair, the lady at your elbow raises her fork. "See ya next year!" Is that an observation or a command? "Next year!" you agree.

WHEN MATT LIBBY'S SEAPLANE CLEARS LAKE MATAGAMON, bearing northwest to Lake Millinocket, the land unfurls below like a topographic map. Long silver lakes and shining outlet streams beget Maine's great northern rivers—Allagash, Aroostook, Penobscot—where salmon and trout spawn in September's chill waters. The plane descends, settling dockside like a goose. First thing, you grab your rod case and hike to a pond to sate your fish lust. "Those little beaver ponds get wicked overpopulated," Matt says. Six- and seven-inch brookies snap at every clumsy cast. When you return with two small ones for supper, Matt observes, "A six-inch trout tastes just as good as a fourteen-incher." That evening, you study the trophy catches on the lodge walls, and try to master a competitive urge. First light finds you a hundred yards from your cabin,

Gone Fishing

LIBBY CAMPS, LAKE MILLINOCKET, TOWNSHIP 8, RANGE 9

You go where the fish go—and instinct drives the trout and salmon ever upstream to spawn in Maine's northern interior.

whipping the line overhead. There is no perfect cast, only the infinite permutations of line and fly, wind and water. Fishing is neither art nor will. Fishing simply is. When you're finally empty of desire—one day or three days or a week later—Matt flies you up-country to an anonymous still water where sea-run salmon are staging. "I'd never tell a fish hog about a good hole," he says. It's a compliment. As he prepares to leave you until evening, he shouts "white wolf" over the engine's roar and lifts off with a belch of blue smoke. You follow his advice, and tie on that fly. A spawner snaps at your third cast. He tears away, then turns and swims straight for you faster than you can reel. Leaping in a rainbow arc, he shakes the hook. That night, after Ellen Libby's blueberry pie, the stories begin beneath the lodge's moose-horn chandeliers. Yours is about the one that got away, and that's just fine.

Libby Camps has offered rustic comfort to sportsmen in the wilds of the north woods since 1890. Eight cabins of hand-peeled logs surround the main lodge on Lake Millinocket.

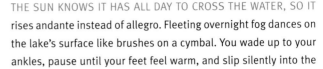

THE SUN KNOWS IT HAS ALL DAY TO CROSS THE WATER, SO IT rises andante instead of allegro. Fleeting overnight fog dances on the lake's surface like brushes on a cymbal. You wade up to your ankles, pause until your feet feel warm, and slip silently into the water for a swim. A Broadway tune from the night before becomes your metronome: a long reach on one beat, a hard pull on the next. The aroma of coffee wafts over the water from shore. After breakfast, you linger over one last cup, eavesdropping on some kitchen staffers who are practicing scales while washing dishes. You could settle into indolence, but instead you push off in a canoe to practice some J-strokes and watch the sun strike the faces of the Presidentials. Much later, you recline in a lakeside chaise longue in the grip of a paperback saga. The piping of a flutist wafts

Lakeside Lyric

QUISISANA RESORT, KEZAR LAKE, WESTERN MAINE

From the opening notes of birdsong to the silent applause of starlight, summer throbs with its own soundtrack at Quisisana.

through the woods, her embouchure so accomplished it could make Pan weep with envy. Just as the golden light of late afternoon begins to cast slanted shadows, a trio made up of a violin, flute, and cello launches into Mozart on a grassy point at the water's edge. Cocktail glasses clink in percussion until the assembly heads in to eat. After serving a prime-rib dinner, the waiters and waitresses gather to sing birthday greetings in four-part harmony. You cover one ear to find the pitch and join in. Later, in the music hall, a chambermaid steps to the piano. Transformed like Cinderella, she overwhelms the audience with Rachmaninoff. Momentarily stunned silence shatters in delighted applause. After a reception with cookies and lemonade, you stroll back through the lighted pinewoods to your cottage. A loon begins its manic call. It's E-minor, you're pretty sure.

The breath of summer swings between inspiration and exhilaration. The lake, the woods, and the skillful playing of young musicians all resolve in a major chord of simple joy.

TEN O'CLOCK AND, READY OR NOT, THE CHILDREN'S BIKE BRIGADE LEADS OFF THE parade, streamers flying. Old Glory waves from every flagpole and car antenna, and the town is dressed in red, white, and blue. Behind the bicycles come the Civil War re-enactors and the air force color guard, half a dozen neighborhood floats, and a small armada of antique cars honking away. The marchers snake past the reviewing stand in front of the library and on to Dodge's store, where spectators burst into applause, and the Hollis Dixieland Band breaks into "Stars and Stripes Forever." A contingent of antique fire trucks brings up the rear with bells ringing and high-spirited firemen zapping bystanders with squirt guns. Onlookers fall in behind as the parade turns at the town green and continues up Goffstown Road to the 4-H Fairgrounds. At the podium a speaker recalls the truths we hold to be self-evident. A singer holds the high

The Pursuit of Happiness

FOURTH OF JULY IN NEW BOSTON, NEW HAMPSHIRE

The pageantry of the past converges with summer's ripeness as country folk gather together to celebrate the nation's birthday.

note on the word "free" in the national anthem. Just as every patriot is choking up, the first report fires from the Molly Stark cannon. Artillerymen load a fresh charge and ram it home; Old Molly booms again. The smell of black powder wafts across the grounds. Uncle Sam stands at rigid attention, and the scouts give their two- and three-fingered salutes. Then the pursuit of happiness begins with a down-and-dirty mud-volleyball tournament and a watermelon-eating contest. Hamburgers sizzle and chickens pop and spit on barbecues. Teenagers take turns operating the 19th-century fire pumper. Fiddle music swirls above the din, and a John Deere squares off against a Toro in the lawn-tractor pull. Throughout the long twilight, carloads of families stream into the fairgrounds. At 9:15, red rockets glare, bombs burst in air, and through the night, our flag is still there.

Friendly competitions—mud volleyball, horse
pulling—mark New Hampshire's Independence
Day. Cooperation—a staunch militia, a volunteer
fire brigade—is just as dear.

The Poet's World

ALONG THE ROBERT FROST MEMORIAL HIGHWAY IN CENTRAL VERMONT

NOBODY REMEMBERS IF IT WAS CHOCOLATE OR VANILLA HE PREFERRED, BUT ON SWELTERING summer days Robert Frost would walk through the doors of Lyon's Drugstore, plop down on a stool at the marble counter, and order up an ice cream soda. His poet's laurels set aside, he'd suck the glass's bottom dry, just like any man. For a score of years and more, Frost fixed his cold eye and tart tongue on this plainspoken landscape of high-country pasture and gnarled orchards, where forest has overtaken farm. You can conjure the man with the names of the places: Middlebury, Bread Loaf, Rochester, Ripton. "All great literature begins in geography," he liked to say, meaning every word. From his cabin at the back of Homer Noble's farm, Frost wrestled with his angel over words, and vanquished, he'd set out to walk these woods. Age never dimmed those ice-blue eyes or stopped the voice that matched a name to every plant

he "botanized." You follow down the path he took. Look carefully: you'll find the poet in every sight he put to verse. The old man's apples still blush and ripen. No ladder bends the boughs, but the fruit falls just the same, and a doe comes to browse at dusk, grateful and unquestioning. Jostled just a bit askew by years of freeze and thaw, the stone wall has its gaps but stands in outline still. No neighbors need be fenced out now, nor author's yearnings kept fenced in. Listen well. Frost's voice is in the wind, the stones, the little bird who cries "killdeer!" and flies up startled from the stubble field. Deep in a yellow wood, past the rushing water of the falls, two roads diverge, demanding that you choose.

Robert Frost embraced the countryside of rural New England, drawing his poetic vigor from the pastoral landscape.

"WALK! WE'RE JUDGING THE WALK!" THE ANNOUNCER BARKS THROUGH a megaphone. As if a carousel had come to life, a dozen horses straighten their necks and circle the ring, sleigh bells tinkling as hooves clop on the hard-packed snow. "Trot! The working trot!" In a dozen sleighs drivers click their tongues, and the horses change gait. A black Arabian gelding arches his tail and picks up his hooves in a rhythmic prance. Even the muscular, mottled-gray Percheron—a dobbin bred for the plow and the sledge—seems to be wearing dancing shoes. "Walk! Walk!" They all slow down so the judge can scrutinize the box sleigh, the Portland cutter, and the two-section bob sleigh that can pivot around turns. This is the Currier & Ives Class of a Green Mountain Horse Association sleigh rally. If you squint, you can imagine having

Jingle Bells

OPEN SLEIGHS IN SOUTH WOODSTOCK, VERMONT

This driver's buggy whip is just for show. Sleigh-rally horses are well-trained equine athletes that know all their paces.

slipped back into the 19th century. The judge, draped in an antique beaver coat, lets no detail escape. She scrutinizes a gentleman's top hat and his wife's beribboned bonnet. She catalogs period accoutrements: sand weights sewn into the hem of a lap robe, a buffalo-hide throw, brass (instead of nickel) harness fittings. Drivers beam as the winners are announced, the ribbons are awarded, and the spectators applaud with vigor. "I'm just a sleigh rally groupie," says a retired woman from New York. She laughs. "It's more fun than ice-fishing." Teams take a break so that the drivers can change into warmer, modern garb before navigating traffic cones on the obstacle course. Only one sleigh spills, and no one is hurt. The horses prick up their ears in excitement for the open-field finale. The Morgan mare gets frisky, as if she sniffs green grass in the icy breeze. She breaks into a joyful trot, over the river and through the woods.

"Dashing through the snow / In a one-horse
open sleigh / O'er the fields we go /
Laughing all the way"—you can still have
the "Jingle Bells" experience described in
James Lord Pierpont's 1859 lyrics.

All the Details

Northern New England is America's gentle wilderness. Its people have never needed to conquer it so much as to enjoy it. Perhaps that's why Vermont's longest thoroughfare is the Long Trail instead of an interstate highway. Maybe that's why New Hampshire's granite peaks are topped with shelters instead of condos, and why the Maine woods, even after nearly two centuries of logging, are still dense with trees. The region is defined by both its landscapes and its seasons. Spring waterfalls cascade down mountains, sandy beaches seem to go on forever in the late gloaming of summer days. The air turns as crisp as a tart apple in fall, and snow billows over rolling hills in winter. High season stretches from late June through Labor Day, with a second wave during foliage season, mid-September through Columbus Day. Layered clothing is a good idea. Temperatures routinely vary 25-30 degrees Fahrenheit between night and day. They range from single digits to freezing in winter, near-freezing to mid-50s in spring and fall, and 40s to mid-70s in summer.

Northern New England covers 49,083 square miles, with Maine alone accounting for 60 percent of the area. International airports are found in Bangor and Portland, Maine; Manchester, New Hampshire; and Burlington, Vermont. Many travelers, however, fly to Boston's Logan International Airport, New England's largest. A car is essential. Trains and buses won't deliver you to the many pancake breakfasts and church suppers. Without your own vehicle you can't fully explore Maine's peninsulas or earn the bumper sticker "This Car Climbed Mount Washington." Adventures are grouped by region, and the suggested lodgings are often integral to the experience. Unless otherwise stated, properties are open year-round, accept credit cards, and offer rooms with private bath. For more information, contact the Maine Tourism Association, Box 2300, Hallowell, ME 04347-2300, 207/623-0363, www.visitmaine.com; the New Hampshire Division of Travel and Tourism, Box 1856, Concord, NH 03302-1856, 603/271-2665, www.visitnh.gov; and the Vermont Department of Tourism and Marketing, Box 1471, Montpelier, VT 05601-1471, 802/828-3236 or 800/VERMONT, www.travelvermont.com.

Drive carefully—and don't forget to brake for moose! *Grid coordinates, listed after town names in the following section, refer to the maps on pages 81 and 82.*

THE GREEN MOUNTAINS

Two major north–south roads, Route 7 in the west and Route 100 in the east, outline the softly rounded Green Mountains, named for the verdure of their slopes. The main population centers lie along these roads, which

tend to follow river valleys. Between them stands the Green Mountain National Forest (2G-K)–vast tracts of undeveloped hillsides, many of which have reverted to true wilderness since the forest was established in 1932. The lower altitudes of the Green Mountains are notable for their variety of deciduous trees, producing some of the world's most flamboyant fall foliage. The higher altitudes support broad-limbed conifers that snowfall transforms into archetypal winter images.

HIKING FROM HUT TO HUT ON VERMONT'S LONG TRAIL (2K–3E)

Not Just a Walk in the Woods, p. 36

Members of the Green Mountain Club started to blaze the Long Trail in 1910, and by 1931 it stretched 270 mi from Massachusetts to Canada along the main ridge of the Green Mountains. A few hardy souls test their mettle by hiking the Long Trail in a single three- to five-week journey, but because Vermont roads provide many access points, it's easy to hit the trail for a week, a weekend, or even a day. Although segments pass through designated wilderness areas, most of the route is best classified as "backcountry." Approximately 175 mi of side trails augment the Long Trail network. Conditions vary from muddy hemlock marsh to bare rock, from even ground to steep ascents where trekking poles come in handy. Don't set off without *The Long Trail Guide*, published by the Green Mountain Club.

CONTACT: Green Mountain Club (GMC), R.R. 1, Box 650, Waterbury Center, VT 05677, tel. 802/244–7037, www.greenmountainclub.org.

DISTANCES: Beginning at the Massachusetts border—roughly 4 mi north of Route 2 in Williamstown—the Long Trail runs to the frontier with Canada, ending about 5 mi west of North Troy, VT (3E). The segment described on p. 36—Skyline Lodge to Taft Lodge—is one of the most rewarding stretches of high-elevation hiking. Southern access to this section is from the Middlebury Gap trailhead on Route 125, 6.4 mi west of the junction with Route 100 in Hancock (2H). Northern access is from Route 108, 8.2 mi north of the Route 100 junction in Stowe (3F).

HOURS: The Long Trail is open to hikers, skiers, and snowshoers in all seasons at no charge but at their own risk. The main hiking season is early May to early November, but freezing temperatures, hail, and snow aren't unknown in high elevations at both ends of the season. Mud can be a major problem from March through May as well as in November. The GMC Center, on Route 100 between Waterbury (3F) and Stowe, is open daily 9–5 Memorial Day through Columbus Day and weekdays 9–5 the rest of the year.

OPTIONS: The more than 70 overnight sites on the Long Trail are never more than a moderate day's hike apart, and each has a privy and a source of water that must be treated before drinking. Sites vary from tent platforms to three-sided lean-tos to fully enclosed log structures. Bring your own food, overnight gear, and backpacking stove. From early May until early November, resident caretakers maintain some of the more-visited shelters, including the Skyline and Taft lodges, where a $5 fee is charged. All other sites are free. Skyline has an idyllic setting on a hill looking east over Skylight Pond and beyond to the White Mountains (4H–7F). Taft, which sleeps 24, is the trail's largest lodge. It's also one of the oldest: volunteers rebuilt the 1920 log structure in 1996. Two hiker-friendly lodgings make good bases for day treks. Constructed in 1938, the **Inn at Long Trail** is all tree-trunk beams and split-log stairs; its dining room is built around a massive glacial boulder. Hikers and skiers gather for a pint and live music at McGrath's Pub. Rooms in the original inn are basic; newer suites with fireplaces are also available. Follow the Sherburne Pass Trail, adjacent to the inn parking lot, a short distance north to connect to both the Long and Appalachian trails. Rte. 4, Killington, VT 05751, tel. 802/775–7181 or 800/325–2540, fax 802/747–7034, www.innatlongtrail.com. 16 rooms, 5 suites. Restaurant, pub, hot tub, hiking. Double $68–$114 with full breakfast. On 9 acres along Notch Brook in Stowe, the 1936 **Inn at Turner Mill** truly encourages rustic reverie with its exposed wood and stone construction, its log beds, and its handcrafted tables and chairs. Accommodations range from double rooms to four-bedroom suites with living rooms and kitchens (some suites also have fireplaces). From the inn, it's a challenging three-hour hike to the alpine tundra at Mt. Mansfield's summit (3F). 56 Turner Mill La., Stowe, VT 05672, tel. 802/253–2062 or 800/992–0016, www.turnermill.com. 4 rooms, 4 suites. Pool, hiking. Double $55–$110. Full breakfast served summer–fall only.

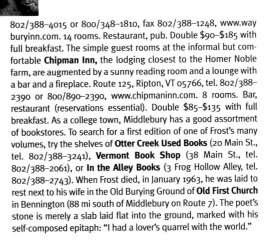

ALONG THE ROBERT FROST MEMORIAL HIGHWAY IN CENTRAL VERMONT (2G–3H)
The Poet's World, p. 74

Although Robert Frost inhabited many parts of New England, his stamp is indelible on the countryside of old farms and second-growth forest near his cabin on the Homer Noble farm (2G) in Ripton. From 1938 to 1962 Frost participated in the writing workshops of the Bread Loaf Writers' Conference, and his summer world consisted of the college community of Middlebury (2G), the buttercup-colored Bread Loaf campus (2H), his little village of Ripton, and the town of Rochester (3H), a few miles south of Hancock (2H) on Route 100. Two miles east of Ripton, on Route 125, the Robert Frost Wayside makes a useful starting point to find some of the poet's other haunts. A dirt road just east of the wayside leads to the Homer Noble farm, which Middlebury College owns and maintains as a memorial to Frost. The poet's cabin is not open to visitors, but you can peek through its windows and walk the grounds. Across Route 125 and a few hundred yards west of the wayside is the Robert Frost Interpretive Trail, an easy 1-mi loop through a variety of landscapes akin to those that inspired Frost. Alert walkers will find wild blueberries in late July and early August.

CONTACT: Addison County Area Information, 2 Court St., Rte. 7, Middlebury, VT 05753, tel. 802/388–7951 or 800/SEE–VER-MONT, www.midvermont.com.

DISTANCES: The Robert Frost Memorial Highway is the section of Route 125 between East Middlebury and Hancock. Middlebury is 35 mi south of Burlington (2F), on Route 7. Hancock is 19 mi east, at the intersection of Route 125 and Route 100.

OPTIONS: Lyon's Drugstore is gone, but the circa 1940 marble soda fountain and its chrome stools have been installed next door at the **Rochester Café,** which is open daily 7–4. Main St., Rochester, tel. 802/767–4302. In lively Middlebury, the **Swift House Inn** has a range of distinctively decorated rooms, some with fireplaces and terraces, in three historic buildings. The largest and most luxurious accommodations are in the 1886 carriage house. 25 Stewart La., Middlebury, VT 05753, tel. 802/388–9925, fax 802/388–9927, www.swifthouseinn.com. 21 rooms. Bar, sauna, steam room. Double $90–$195 with Continental breakfast. For a rural experience, try the **Waybury Inn.** Rooms are furnished in late Victorian style; the restaurant offers country cooking. Route 125, East Middlebury, VT 05753, tel.

802/388–4015 or 800/348–1810, fax 802/388–1248, www.way buryinn.com. 14 rooms. Restaurant, pub. Double $90–$185 with full breakfast. The simple guest rooms at the informal but comfortable **Chipman Inn,** the lodging closest to the Homer Noble farm, are augmented by a sunny reading room and a lounge with a bar and a fireplace. Route 125, Ripton, VT 05766, tel. 802/388–2390 or 800/890–2390, www.chipmaninn.com. 8 rooms. Bar, restaurant (reservations essential). Double $85–$135 with full breakfast. As a college town, Middlebury has a good assortment of bookstores. To search for a first edition of one of Frost's many volumes, try the shelves of **Otter Creek Used Books** (20 Main St., tel. 802/388–3241), **Vermont Book Shop** (38 Main St., tel. 802/388–2061), or **In the Alley Books** (3 Frog Hollow Alley, tel. 802/388–2743). When Frost died, in January 1963, he was laid to rest next to his wife in the Old Burying Ground of **Old First Church** in Bennington (88 mi south of Middlebury on Route 7). The poet's stone is merely a slab laid flat into the ground, marked with his self-composed epitaph: "I had a lover's quarrel with the world."

MAPLE FESTIVAL, WHITINGHAM, VERMONT (2K)
How Sweet It Is, p. 42

About 37% of this country's maple syrup comes from Vermont, making that state the nation's largest producer. Whitingham holds the state's only maple festival during the actual sugaring season, which is roughly the month of March and the first 10 days of April. In addition to sugarhouse visits, Whitingham's festival has children's activities, maple-cooking demonstrations, a maple-sugar recipe contest, a pancake breakfast, a sugar-on-snow dinner, a crafts fair, and a quilt raffle.

CONTACT: Maple Sugar Festival, Whitingham Town Office, Whitingham, VT 05361, tel. 802/368–7887, www.whiting hammaplefest.com.

DISTANCES: Whitingham is on Route 100, 23 mi northwest of Greenfield, MA (4K), via Routes 2 and 112.

PRICES/HOURS: The maple festival takes place on the last full weekend in March that does not coincide with Easter. Sugarhouses are open 10–4. All activities are free except for the pancake breakfast ($5) and the sugar-on-snow dinner ($8).

OPTIONS: The best lodging options are in or near Jacksonville, a village of the town of Whitingham. Bill and Patti Pusey tap 700 trees and make their own maple syrup at **Shearer Hill Farm Bed**

and Breakfast. Guests are encouraged to lend a hand. This small working farm, a few miles out along dirt roads from Jacksonville, has simply decorated but spacious guest rooms—three in the farmhouse, three more in a carriage house. A warm, inviting common room has a wood-burning stove, large windows opening on scenic vistas, and lots of comfortable seating. Shearer Hill Rd., Box 1453, Wilmington, VT 05363, tel. 802/464-3253 or 800/437-3104, www.shearerhillfarm.com. 6 rooms. Breakfast room. Double $90 with full breakfast; 20% discount for stays of two or more nights during sugaring season. The Candlelight Bed & Breakfast occupies a circa-1850 farmhouse above a big bend in the road just south of Jacksonville center. Rooms have country quilts, brass or antique wooden beds, wingback chairs, fireplaces or woodstoves. 3358 Rte. 100, Jacksonville, VT 05342, tel. 802/368-2004, www.candlelightbandb.com. 3 rooms. Breakfast room. Double $85–$95 with full breakfast.

GREEN MOUNTAINS HIGHLIGHTS

Route 100, which runs up the middle of Vermont between mountain ridges, is one of the state's finest foliage highways. Along the road is Killington (2I), Vermont's largest outdoors center, with skiing in winter at Killington Basin Ski Area and Pico Peak Ski Area and 50 mi of trails to hike in summer and fall. Killington also maintains 41 mi of mountain-biking trails during "hard sledding" (i.e., snow-free) parts of the year. The towns of Warren (2G) and Waitsfield (3G), on Route 100, may have a bucolic simplicity, but the urbanites who visit them are sophisticated. They come to enjoy the rugged pleasures of Mad River Glen ski area and the once-chic ski resort of Sugarbush, favored by mature skiers for its classic terrain. In March, Mad River Glen hosts the world's oldest and largest gathering of backcountry telemark skiers.

THE CONNECTICUT RIVER VALLEY

The Connecticut River forms much of the boundary between Vermont and New Hampshire, with crossings every few miles. The most picturesque is the 460-ft Cornish-Windsor Bridge—the longest two-span covered wooden bridge in the United States—which links Cornish, NH (4I), and Windsor, VT (3I). The valley is easy to access from the south, as I-91 follows the Vermont side of the river from the Massachusetts border north as far as Barnet. But the riverside roads of Route 5 in Vermont and Route 12 in New Hampshire are more scenic, if more congested.

WILD GAME CHURCH SUPPER IN BRADFORD, VERMONT (4G)

Please Pass the Pheasant Pâté, p. 60

Bradford's game supper, dubbed the "Super Bowl of church suppers" by Calvin Trillin, is renowned for the variety of game served, the different preparations, and the boundless community spirit behind the event. "You get the kid who used to come with his parents, and now he's bringing his own kids. That's neat," observes Gary Tomlinson, who co-chaired the event from 1978 to 1986. The supper is held on the Saturday before Thanksgiving, and ticket sales are capped at 900–1,000. Diners have come from 44 states and several foreign countries. Profits maintain the Congregational church, a gleaming white edifice constructed in 1876 to loom larger than the Methodist church across the street. The Methodists don't hold a grudge, loaning their kitchen for baking the pheasant-rice casseroles.

CONTACT: Bradford Annual Wild Game Supper, c/o Mrs. Raymond Green, 217 N. Main St., Bradford, VT 05033, tel. 802/222-5913 (co-chair Penny Randall) mistwebdesign.com/ucc.html. Reservation request must not be postmarked before mid-October.

DISTANCES: Bradford, Vermont, is off I-91 at Exit 16, 148 mi north of Springfield, MA (4K), and 28 mi north of White River Junction, VT (4I).

OPTIONS: Lodging in Bradford is limited to the bare-bones-but-immaculate Bradford Motel, U.S. 5, Bradford, VT 05033, tel. 802/222-4467. 16 rooms. Double $37–$58. A few miles south, the Silver Maple Lodge offers guest rooms in an 18th-century farmhouse or knotty-pine–paneled cottages from the early days of auto touring. The three cottage rooms have working fireplaces; two have kitchenettes. U.S. 5, Fairlee, VT 05045, tel. 802/333-4326 or 800/666-1946, www.silvermaplelodge.com. 15 rooms (two share bath). Double $69–$89 with Continental breakfast. An elegant chalet on a wooded mountainside north of Bradford, the Whipple-Tree Bed & Breakfast has large windows and views of the distant White Mountains. Rooms are spacious and modern, but you'll probably spend more time relaxing in front of the lounge's massive stone fireplace. 487 Stevens Pl., Wells River, VT 05081, tel. 802/429-2076 or 800/466-4097, fax 802/ 429-2858, www.whipple tree.com. 6 rooms. Exercise equipment, hot tub, cross-country skiing. Double $140–$190 with full breakfast.

MOUNTAIN VIEW FARM, EAST BURKE, NORTHEAST KINGDOM, VERMONT (4F)
King of the Hill, p. 56

Elmer A. Darling, an East Burke native, established the Mountain View Farm in 1883. By the turn of the century, the gentleman farmer's herd of Jersey cattle enabled him to stock his Fifth Avenue Hotel in New York with plenty of milk, butter, and cheese. Darling also bred champion Morgan horses, stabling them in the circa-1912 red barn with a giant clock above its door. A gracious inn and restaurant occupy the redbrick structure that was once the creamery, and the original farmhouse has two suites. Hayrides and sleigh rides are available on the property, which includes the central 440 acres of the original 8,000-acre estate. Guests are also encouraged to explore the area on hikes and on mountain-bike, snowshoe, or cross-country-skiing excursions.

CONTACT: Inn at Mountain View Farm, Darling Hill Rd., Box 355, East Burke, VT 05832, tel. 802/626–9924 or 800/572–4509, www.innmtnview.com.

DISTANCES: East Burke is 15 mi from St. Johnsbury, VT (4F), and 7 mi from Exit 23 off I–91.

PRICES/HOURS: The Inn at Mountain View Farm is open year-round. 9 rooms, 1 suite in creamery building, 2 suites in farmhouse. Restaurant, hiking, cross-country skiing. Double $115–$370 with full breakfast.

OPTIONS: A little more than a mile west of the Inn at Mountain View Farm, the **Wildflower Inn** was originally part of the Darling property. Rooms are distributed among four buildings, including a carriage house, an old schoolhouse, and a farmhouse. Darling Hill Rd., Lyndonville, VT 05851, tel. 800/627–8310, www.wildflowerinn.com. 10 rooms, 11 suites. Restaurant, tennis court, pool, basketball courts, volleyball, meeting rooms. Double $95–$280 with full breakfast. Both the Mountain View Farm and Wildflower inns are on the **Kingdom Trails** (www.kingdomtrails.org) network of more than 100 mi of interconnected trails for hiking, mountain biking, and cross-country skiing. To rent mountain bikes, visit **East Burke Sports,** Rte. 114, East Burke, VT 05832, tel. 802/626–3215.

OPEN SLEIGHS IN SOUTH WOODSTOCK, VERMONT (3I)
Jingle Bells, p. 76

Home of the Green Mountain Horse Association (GMHA), tiny South Woodstock functions as Vermont's equestrian capital. Residents joke that the town has more horses than registered automobiles. Spectators are welcome at the year-round competitive riding and driving events held at the GMHA's grounds. Paul Kendall of Kedron Valley Stables offers sleigh rides in winter. Trips follow streambeds and woods trails. Some riders like to bring wine to sip, as well as apples or carrots for the horses.

CONTACTS: Green Mountain Horse Association, Rte. 106, Box 8, South Woodstock, VT 05071, tel. 802/457–1509, fax 802/457–4471, www.gmhainc.org. **Kedron Valley Stables,** Rte. 106, South Woodstock, VT 05071, tel. 802/457–1480 or 800/225–6301, fax 802/457–3029, www.kedron.com.

DISTANCES: South Woodstock is 5 mi south of Woodstock, VT (3I), on Route 106. Woodstock is 20 mi west of White River Junction on Route 4.

PRICES/HOURS: Admission to GMHA sleigh rallies is free; contact the association for schedules. Kedron Valley Stables offers sleigh rides daily, conditions permitting. Reserve at least one day in advance. Rates are $65 for one to three riders, $90 for four to nine riders, $10 per person for 10 or more.

OPTIONS: Built in the 1820s as a stagecoach stop, the **Kedron Valley Inn** is one of Vermont's oldest hostelries. Many rooms have fireplaces or woodstoves as well as canopy beds. Heirloom quilts and hooked rugs abound. The Tavern restaurant serves updated New England fare. Rte. 106, South Woodstock, VT 05071, tel. 802/457–1473 or 800/836–1193, fax 802/457–4469, www.kedronvalleyinn.com. 24 rooms, 4 suites. Restaurant, bar, lake. Double $135–$260 with full breakfast, plus 15% service charge. A few miles from the horse action is the 1890 mansion that is now the **Jackson House Inn & Restaurant**. Rooms are furnished with Victorian, French Empire, or New England country antiques. The dining room, which has a cathedral ceiling and a granite hearth, overlooks a 5-acre garden. Polished New American cuisine dominates the fixed-price menu. 114-3 Senior La., Woodstock, VT 05091, tel. 802/457–2065 or 800/448–1890, fax 802/457–9290, www.jacksonhouse.com. 9 rooms, 6 suites. Restaurant, bar, pond. Double $195–$380 with full breakfast and evening hors d'oeuvres, plus 10% service charge.

CONNECTICUT RIVER VALLEY HIGHLIGHTS
With northern New England's richest soil, the Connecticut River Valley is dotted with picturesque farms and villages. The Saint-Gaudens National Historic Site in **Cornish**, NH, captures the well-heeled bohemian idyll of the artists and writers who populated the area at the turn of the last century. Saint-Gaudens's own neoclassical sculptures, however, are the real stars. **Hanover**, NH (4I), was conceived as a center of culture in the wilderness even when Dartmouth College was founded in 1769. Be sure to see the Orozco murals at the Baker Library and the Abyssinian bas-reliefs at the Hood Museum of Art. Dartmouth's Hopkins Center for Performing Arts books a steady stream of concerts and plays. The Vermont side of the river is a study in contrasts. Well buffed by Rockefeller millions, **Woodstock** is home to the Billings Farm & Museum, showcasing early "scientific farming," as well as many boutiques and galleries. **St. Johnsbury** remains an outpost of Vermont's counterculture. The Fairbanks Museum and Planetarium in "St. Jay" is a marvel of taxidermy, with so many stuffed polar bears that the institution adopted the beast for its emblem.

NEW HAMPSHIRE FARMLAND

Adventurers to northern New England often neglect southwestern New Hampshire's rolling green pastureland. Its pleasures lie in the friendly charms of small-town life, a history of rugged individualism, and a sense of being removed in time as well as distance from modern urban life. Although arterial Route 101 runs east–west across the area's southern edge, and I–93 and I–89 define its eastern and northern boundaries, a spiderweb of small roads encourages wandering through a rural landscape little altered in the last century.

FOURTH OF JULY IN NEW BOSTON, NEW HAMPSHIRE *(5K)*
The Pursuit of Happiness, p. 70

The firing of the Molly Stark cannon—named after General John Stark's wife and fondly called Old Molly—is central to New Boston's Independence Day celebrations. The general gave the cannon to the New Boston Artillery Company of the Ninth Regiment of the New Hampshire Militia in recognition of the unit's key role in the Revolutionary War's Battle of Bennington. The

brass 4-pounder was originally cast by the French in 1743, and captured by the British in Québec. American rebels took it from the British at Bennington on August 15, 1777. Among the other Fourth of July events are a barn dance, a fiddling contest, a horse-pulling competition, and a battle-skills demonstration by the Civil War re-enactors of New Hampshire Cavalry K.

CONTACT: New Boston Fourth of July Association, Box 272, New Boston, NH 03070, no phone, www.new-boston.nh.us.

DISTANCES: New Boston is 15 mi west of Manchester, NH (5J–6K), via Routes 114 and 13.

OPTIONS: Some of the area's choice inns are 16 mi north of New Boston (5K) on Routes 77 and 114 in Henniker (5J). Over the years the central, foursquare building of the **Colby Hill Inn** has been a stagecoach tavern, a hall where temperance advocates met, the main house of a huge farm, and, since 1959, an inn. Each guest room has a sleigh, canopy, brass, or iron bed as well as a comfortable chair and a good reading light. The restaurant, a regional dining destination, emphasizes contemporary American cooking using seasonal local products. The Oaks (Rte. 114, village center), Box 779, Henniker, NH 03242, tel. 603/428–3281 or 800/531–0330, fax 603/428–9218, www.colbyhillinn.com. 16 rooms. Restaurant, pool. Double $110–$200 with full breakfast. The **Meeting House** is a small inn occupying the circa-1840 town meeting building near Pat's Peak Ski Area. Each cozy, country-style guest room has a table with chairs so you can enjoy the breakfast that's delivered in a picnic basket. The restaurant is a dramatic transformation of a 200-year-old barn; a superb wine list complements the contemporary American dishes. 35 Flanders Rd., Henniker, NH 03242, tel. 603/428–3228, fax 603/428–6334, www.meetinghouseinn.com. 6 rooms. Restaurant. Double $85–$125 with full breakfast.

SHAKER COMMUNITIES IN ENFIELD AND CANTERBURY, NEW HAMPSHIRE *(4I, 5I)*
Peace on Earth, p. 28

Founded at the end of the 18th century, Enfield and Canterbury were among the earliest of the Shaker communities that spread from Maine to Florida and west to Kentucky. Following the teachings of founder Mother Ann Lee, members of the United Society of Believers in Christ's First and Second Appearing—commonly called Shakers in reference to their ecstatic twitching during worship—owned goods in common, believed in pacifism, and practiced celibacy and equality of the sexes. The Shakers numbered about 6,000 at their peak in the late 1850s and were known for many practical innovations, including the revolving oven, packaged garden seeds, the industrial washing machine, the flat broom, and furniture noted for its comfort and lack of ornament. Dependent on converts, the sect's numbers dwindled after the Civil War. In 1927 the few remaining Enfield Shakers sold their property and joined Canterbury, where the last sister died in 1992 at age 96. Canterbury Shaker Village, a museum with 23 buildings, shows the breadth of community life. The Enfield Shaker Museum lacks an intact village, but the 1818 dairy/laundry building displays furniture and other crafts, and you can hike to the worship site on Mt. Assurance. Enfield's pièce de résistance is the six-story Great Stone Dwelling, the largest Shaker main dwelling ever built and now the Shaker Inn.

CONTACT: Canterbury Shaker Village, Canterbury, NH 03324, tel. 603/783–9511, www.shakers.org. **Enfield Shaker Museum**, 24 Caleb Dyer La., Enfield, NH 03748, tel. 603/632–4346, www.shakermuseum.org.

DISTANCES: Canterbury Shaker Village is about 15 mi north of Concord, NH (5J); take Exit 18 off I–93 and follow the signs. Enfield Shaker Museum is on Route 4A in Enfield, NH, 12 mi southeast of Hanover, NH. Take Exit 17 off I–89, and follow Route 4 east to Route 4A. The drive between the two villages on Routes 4 and 4A traverses a landscape of 19th-century upland farms and village greens.

PRICES/HOURS: Canterbury Shaker Village is open May–October, daily 10–5; April, November, and December, weekends 10–5. Admission is $10. Canterbury's Creamery Restaurant, serving Shaker cuisine, is open for lunch all days the village is open. Four-course dinners are served May–October on Friday and Saturday; April, November, and December only on Saturday (reservations required). Enfield Shaker Museum is open Memorial Day weekend–October, daily 10–5; November till Christmas, Friday 4–7, Saturday 10–4, and Sunday noon–4; January–Memorial Day weekend, Saturday 10–4 and Sunday noon–4. Admission is $7.

OPTIONS: The **Shaker Inn**'s guest rooms are in the sleeping chambers of Enfield's Great Stone Dwelling. Shaker-style furniture complements the original built-in cabinetry, and private bathrooms have been discreetly added. The inn's restaurant serves Shaker-inspired dishes seasoned with herbs from the museum's garden. 447 Rte. 4A, Enfield, NH 03748, tel.

603/632–7810 or 888/707–4257, fax 603/632-7922, www.theshakerinn.com. 24 rooms. Restaurant, bar, beach. Double $105–$155 with full breakfast. Best lodging choices near Canterbury are in Concord, including **Best Western Concord Inn & Suites**, 97 Hall St., Concord, NH 03301, tel. 603/228–4300, fax 603/228–4301, www.bestwestern.com/concordinnandsuites. 66 rooms. Pool, sauna, spa, fitness center. Double $50–$99 with Continental breakfast. The last remaining Shakers live at **Sabbathday Lake** in New Gloucester, ME (8H), tel. 207/926–4597, www.shaker.lib.me.us. The community, which is 20 mi north of Portland on Route 26, maintains a museum, open Memorial Day–Columbus Day, Monday–Saturday 10:30–4:30. Admission is $6.

PUMPKIN FESTIVAL, KEENE, NEW HAMPSHIRE (4K)
City of Lights, p. 48

The Pumpkin Festival holds the Guinness world record for most lit jack-o'-lanterns: more than 23,000. Pumpkins line the sidewalks throughout downtown Keene, but the most impressive arrays are on 40-ft-high scaffolds at all the approaches to the central shopping area. Festival highlights include a midday costume parade, hay and pony rides, and food booths proffering almost every sweet that can be made from pumpkins or apples. After the official jack-o'-lantern tally is announced at 8 PM, the sky explodes with fireworks. Book lodging far in advance; by the week before the festival, the nearest available rooms are usually 50 mi or more from town.

CONTACT: Center Stage, 39 Central Sq., #305, Keene, NH 03431, tel. 603/358-5344, fax 603/358-6531, www.centerstagenh.com.

DISTANCES: Keene, NH, is 17 mi east of Exit 3 off I–91 in Putney, VT (3K). Exit 3 is 61 mi north of Springfield, MA.

PRICES/HOURS: The Pumpkin Festival takes place 10–10 on the last Saturday in October. Admission and parking are free, and shuttle buses transport you to and from outlying lots.

OPTIONS: A stay at the redbrick **E. F. Lane Hotel**, an 1890s structure, puts you close to all the festival action. The windows of its clublike Goodnow Parlor look out onto Main Street. Guest rooms, however, are quiet retreats done in dark woods and warm colors that evoke a country-squire elegance. Pumpkin Festival weekend requires a two-night minimum stay. 30 Main St., Keene, NH 03431, tel. 603/357-7070 or 888/300-5056, fax 603/357-7075, www.someplacesdifferent.com. 31 rooms, 9 suites. Restaurant, bar, Internet. Double $139–$285. Harvest season becomes palpable at the **Inn at Valley Farms,** a 1774 home on a 105-acre organic farm. You can carve one of the farm's pumpkins to present at the festival. Farmhouse guests enjoy a breakfast prepared with the inn's own eggs, honey, maple syrup, and herbs. Guest rooms are furnished in a country Victorian style; all have four-poster beds. The three-bedroom cottages have full kitchens. 633 Wentworth Rd., Walpole, NH 03608, tel. 603/756–2855 or 877/327–2855, fax 603/756–2865, www.innatvalleyfarms.com. 2 rooms, 1 suite, 2 cottages. Games room. Double $95–$160 with full breakfast in farmhouse, Continental breakfast in cottages. Across the road from the Inn at Valley Farms is **Alyson's Apple Orchards**. Stop by to select heirloom apples you'll never see at supermarkets. Wentworth Rd., Walpole, NH, tel. 603/756–9090.

NEW HAMPSHIRE FARMLAND HIGHLIGHTS
Five standing covered bridges make the little town of **Swanzey** (4K), 14 mi south of Keene, New England's unofficial covered-bridge capital. The Greater Keene Chamber of Commerce supplies a free map of the bridges, which were built between 1789 and 1864. The region's two major cities each have a significant museum worth a short detour. The Museum of New Hampshire History in **Concord**, not far from Canterbury Shaker Village, has strong collections of Colonial and Federal furniture and an engaging exhibit on the Concord Coach, the vehicle that opened the American West to civilized travel. The Currier Gallery of Art in **Manchester** also has New Hampshire furniture, as well as American and European painting.

THE WHITE MOUNTAINS

The White Mountains have intrigued visitors since 1508, when explorer Giovanni da Verrazano marveled over "high mountains within the land" as he sailed through the Gulf of Maine. Most of the Whites stand less than 6,000 ft, but they rise steeply from near sea level, producing peaks and valleys nearly as precipitous as those of the Alps. And like the Alps, the Whites have splendid hiking trails and dramatic ski slopes. Good roads link the region's sights and settlements. Condo- and factory-outlet–lined Route 16 runs up the eastern side of the mountains, and I-93 runs up the western edge through Franconia Notch (5G). Only a few roads run east–west through the mountains: Routes 112 (the Kancamagus Highway), 302, and 2.

FOLIAGE SEASON ON NEW HAMPSHIRE'S KANCAMAGUS HIGHWAY (5G–6H)
Drivers Wanted, p. 18

Shorter days and colder nights after the autumnal equinox generally ensure intense displays of yellow, orange, and red foliage at the end of September and through most of October. Although much of the White Mountain National Forest is covered with an evergreen climax forest, the slopes along the Kancamagus Highway were logged recently enough that birch, beech, maples, ash, aspen, cherry, oak, alder, and tupelo explode in this mixed palette. Road builders didn't conquer the area's mountain passes until 1959, and the route wasn't entirely paved until 1962. When the U.S. Forest Service began cataloging scenic byways, its exceptional fall-foliage display guaranteed the "Kanc" a spot at the top of the list. To avoid October's bumper-to-bumper traffic, try to travel on a weekday. Head west to east nonstop for the exhilaration of the drive, then retrace your route to stop for walks in the woods. A short stroll up a logging road at the midpoint leads to Sabbaday Falls, a sequence of cataracts in a deep grotto that might have been the haunt of a Maxfield Parrish nymph. In contrast, the Boulder Loop Trail near Covered Bridge Campground at Lower Falls traverses a glacier-carved landscape, with long mountain views from the Ledges, a precipice 200 ft above the Swift River (6–7G). Rangers at the Saco District Office on the road's eastern end can offer advice about more challenging trails. The Norman B. Fadden Information Center, on the road's western end, sells trail maps and guides.

CONTACTS: National Recreation Reservation Service (for campground reservations), tel. 518/885–3639 or 877/444–6777, www.ReserveUSA.com. **New Hampshire Foliage Hotline,** tel. 800/258–3608 in Sept.–Oct. only. **Norman B. Fadden Information Center,** Rte. 112 (Exit 32 off I–93), Lincoln, NH, no phone. **White Mountain National Forest, Saco District Office,** 33 Kancamagus Hwy., Conway, NH 03818, tel. 603/447–5448.

DISTANCES: Lincoln, NH (5G), 130 mi north of Boston, marks the western end of the Kancamagus. Conway, NH (6H), 77 mi north of Portsmouth, NH (7J), is its eastern terminus.

PRICES/HOURS: If you expect to park for more than 15 minutes along the Kanc, pick up a White Mountain National Forest parking permit at the Saco District Office (open year-round, Mon. 9–4:30 and Tues.–Sun. 8:30–4:30) or the Norman B. Fadden Information Center (open year-round, daily 8:30–5). A permit good for one to seven days costs $5; $20 buys one that's good for a year.

OPTIONS: For full immersion in the autumn landscape, spend the night in one of the six Kancamagus Highway campgrounds operated by the White Mountain National Forest. Sites are suitable for tents or RVs, and Jigger Johnson, the largest campground, has hot showers. Big Rock and Hancock are open year-round. Blackberry Crossing, Covered Bridge, Jigger Johnson, and Passaconaway are open from mid-May to mid-October. Except for Blackberry Crossing, all campgrounds have trailheads for mountain hiking as well as stream or pond access for fishing. In summer and fall, only Covered Bridge accepts reservations (there's an $8.65 reservation fee per site); space at other campgrounds is available on a first-come, first-served basis. Site fees run $14–$16 per day. If you prefer a real roof over your head and a restaurant whose tables are set with linens and crystal, try the **Darby Field Inn & Restaurant,** a few hundred yards off the Kanc near its eastern end. The ground floor of this 1826 homestead is dominated by a grand parlor with a broad fieldstone fireplace. The dining room has a wall of windows framing views of a dozen mountains; some upstairs guest rooms share this panorama. Some have gas fireplaces, and a few have outdoor decks. 185 Chase Hill Rd., Albany, NH 03818, tel. 603/447–2181 or 800/426–4147, fax 603/447–5726, www.darbyfield.com. 14 rooms. Restaurant, bar, pool. Double $120–$210 with full breakfast, $170–$260 with full breakfast and dinner.

BETHLEHEM AND STARK, NEW HAMPSHIRE (5G, 6F)
North Country Christmas, p. 14

Incorporated December 25, 1799, Bethlehem counts Christmas spirit as its birthright. The town celebrates the holiday in the first two weekends of December with evening tram excursions, a crafts bazaar, a church fair, and tours of historic homes decorated for the holidays. Large summer homes sprouted in Bethlehem between the Civil War and the Depression, and many now serve as inns. One of the grandest properties, **The Rocks,** is home to the Society for the Protection of New Hampshire Forests. Roughly 55,000 Christmas trees grow on the 1,300-acre estate; the sale of some of them each year helps to fund the society's conservation work. On weekends, horse-drawn wagons shuttle customers between the main barn and the tree-har-

vesting area (reservations suggested). Rte. 302, Exit 40 off I–93, Bethlehem, NH 03574, tel. 603/444–1600, www.therocks.org. Tiny Stark retains a preindustrial simplicity, where pew-holders worship at the 1853 Union Church (Sunday morning services are held at 8:30), children attend the 1890 village school, and people drive in and out over a two-span, 134-ft, Paddleford-truss covered bridge dating from 1862.

CONTACT: Bethlehem Information Center, Main St., Box 748, Bethlehem, NH 03574, tel. 603/869–3409 or 888/845–1957, www.bethlehemwhitemtns.com.

DISTANCES: Bethlehem is 85 mi north of Concord, NH, following I–93 to Exit 40 east. Stark is 41 mi north of Bethlehem via U.S. 302, U.S. 3, and Rte. 110.

OPTIONS: On the north side of the bridge, the **Stark Village Inn** has a stone fireplace downstairs and three small upstairs guest rooms filled with country furniture, quilts, and homey decorations. 16 Northside Rd., Stark, NH 03582, tel. 603/636–2644. 3 rooms. Double $50 with full breakfast, no credit cards. Bethlehem's **Mulburn Inn,** built in 1908, erects a decorated Christmas tree in each of three lounges, which also have working fireplaces. Rooms are large, decorated in styles from Victorian to art deco. 2370 Main St., Bethlehem, NH 03574, tel. 603/869–3389 or 800/457–9440, www.mulburninn.com. 7 rooms. Hot tub. Double $85–$160 with full breakfast. At the edge of town, the **Adair Country Inn** has rolling grounds and a locally renowned restaurant. Flamboyant hats belonging to the society matron for whom the house was built give the place a quirky élan. Seven of the spacious rooms have fireplaces; all rooms are done in a country Victorian style. The restaurant specializes in robust New American fare, such as rosemary-garlic lamb chops with a spinach, feta, and pine-nut pesto. 80 Guider La., Bethlehem, NH 03574, tel. 603/444–2600 or 888/444–2600, fax 603/444–4823, www.adairinn.com. 9 rooms, 2-bedroom cottage. Restaurant, tennis court, games room. Double $165–$235 with full breakfast and afternoon tea.

WINTER AT NEW HAMPSHIRE'S GRAND MOUNTAIN RESORTS (6E, 6G)
Dress Whites, 22

Many historians claim that tourism in the United States began in the White Mountains when Ethan Allen Crawford cut the first walking trail to the summit of Mt. Washington in 1819, and his father,

Abel, opened an inn at Crawford Notch in the early 1820s. By the time of the Civil War, the White Mountains were dotted with lavish inns, and shortly after the turn of the 20th century the region had 30 grand hotels that each accommodated 250 or more guests. The Mount Washington Hotel & Resort (1902) and the Balsams Grand Resort Hotel (1866) are among the few survivors.

CONTACTS: The **Mount Washington Hotel & Resort,** Rte. 302, Bretton Woods, NH 03585, tel. 603/278–1000 or 800/258–0330, fax 603/278–8838, www.mtwashington.com. The **Balsams Grand Resort Hotel,** Dixville Notch, NH 03576, tel. 603/255–3400 or 800/255–0600, fax 603/255–4221, www.thebalsams.com.

DISTANCES: The Mount Washington is 90 mi north of Concord, NH, via I–93 and Routes 3 and 302. The Balsams is 150 mi north of Concord via I–93 and Routes 3 and 26.

PRICES/HOURS: The Mount Washington is open year-round. 191 rooms, 6 suites. 2 restaurants, bar, lounge, 1 indoor and 1 outdoor pool, swimming in river, 18-hole golf course, 9-hole golf course, 12 tennis courts, hiking, horseback riding, mountain biking, ice skating, cross-country skiing, downhill skiing, snowshoeing. Double $218–$590 with breakfast and dinner. The Balsams is open late May–late Oct. and mid-Dec.–late Mar. 180 rooms, 20 suites. Restaurant, bar, lounge, outdoor pool, 18-hole golf course, 9-hole golf course, 6 tennis courts, lake, hiking, mountain bikes, ice skating, cross-country skiing, downhill skiing, snowboarding, snowshoeing. Late May–late Oct.: double $284–$512 with all meals. Mid-Dec.–late Mar.: double $330–$494 with breakfast and dinner.

OPTIONS: The grand hotels were originally summer-only retreats, but with 200 and 250 inches of natural snowfall, respectively, Bretton Woods and Dixville Notch were destined to become winter-sports centers. As part of the **Bretton Woods Mountain Resort,** the Mount Washington offers access to New Hampshire's largest alpine ski area (76 trails and glades) and 100 km of groomed trails for cross-country skiing, skate skiing, and snowshoeing. Lift fees run $44–$53, and a Nordic trail pass costs $15; skating and snow tubing are free. **The Balsams** offers alpine skiing (14 trails on two slopes), a snowboarding half-pipe, a 95-km cross-country trail system, designated snowshoe trails, and ice skating. All activities and lifts are free to Balsams guests.

WHITE MOUNTAINS HIGHLIGHTS
Mt. Washington (6G) is the literal high point of the White Mountains. Ride to its 6,228-ft summit on the historic cog railway from Bretton Woods or take the auto road up from Glen. (Expert skiers descend this road in winter on backcountry skis with metal edges.) **Wildcat Mountain Ski Area** in Pinkham Notch has the best alpine views in the White Mountains, looking across at Mt. Washington's summit and down on the great scoop of Tuckerman Ravine. **Franconia Notch State Park** (5G), on the western side of the Whites, contains the region's greatest natural anomalies, including the moss-covered walls of the deep cleft known as the Flume, and the natural profile of the Old Man in the Mountain, featured on the New Hampshire license plate.

THE ROCKY COAST

Maine's crumpled, jagged coast between Casco (9H) and Frenchman's bays (13F–12G) is best seen up close. North of Brunswick (9H), the chief thoroughfare is the venerable Route 1, which joins Route 3 between Penobscot Bay (11F) and Mt. Desert Island (12–13F). Almost any road, paved or not, that turns south from Route 1 eventually leads to a seascape of green swells, cliffs and ledges, and spruce-tufted islands. A tiny harbor with a fish shack or a scene from a Marsden Hartley or Edward Hopper painting may be a bonus. The coastal highway demands patience, especially in summer; those frequent turnoffs also mean frequent slowdowns. The water might look inviting, but don't plan to swim. The Labrador current keeps temperatures in the 40s all summer.

LOBSTER HARBORS OF THE MAINE PENINSULAS (9H–13F)
Tail and Claw, p. 32

Three of Maine's best lobster shacks are found at Five Islands on Georgetown Island (9H), Boothbay Harbor on the Boothbay Peninsula (10H), and New Harbor on the Pemaquid Peninsula (10H)—all south or southeast of U.S. 1, a third of the way up the state's coast. The gray clapboard shack of Five Islands Lobster Company overlooks Sheepscot Bay (9–10H), which is dotted with four other islands. Boothbay Region Lobstermen's Co-op is larger and busier, as befits the vacation destination of Boothbay Harbor. Shaw's Fish & Lobster Wharf in New Harbor stands above a fjordlike inlet dense with fishing boats. Signs on the upstairs deck warn you not to feed the gulls and note apologetically that there are no refunds.

CONTACTS: Five Islands Lobster Company, Georgetown, ME 04548, tel. 207/371–2990. **Boothbay Region Lobstermen's Co-op,** 97 Atlantic Ave., Boothbay Harbor, ME 04538, tel. 207/633–4900 or 800/966–1740, www.mainelobstercoop.com. **Shaw's Fish & Lobster Wharf,** Rte. 32, New Harbor, ME 04554, tel. 207/677–2200.

DISTANCES: Southward-pointing spurs off coastal U.S. 1 descend to the lobstering villages on peninsulas between Casco and Penobscot bays. Five Islands lies at the end of Route 127, about 13 mi south of Woolwich (9H). Boothbay Harbor is on Route 27, 11 mi south of Edgecomb (9G). New Harbor is on Route 32. Turn south off Route 1 in Damariscotta (10G) onto Route 130. After 12 mi, turn left onto Route 32 and proceed 1 mi east.

PRICES/HOURS: Most lobster shacks are open mid-May through mid-October. Expect to pay from $8 to $15 for "lobster in the rough," depending on size and season.

OPTIONS: Built as a millionaire's personal retreat in 1904, the blufftop **Grey Havens** inn overlooks a quintessential Maine seascape near Reid State Park (9H). With white rockers on a porch that runs the length of the inn's ocean side and simple Victorian furnishings, Grey Havens retains a turn-of-the-last-century ease and grace. Seguinland Rd., Box 308, Georgetown, ME 04548, tel. 207/371–2616 or 800/431–2316, fax 207/371–2274, www.greyhavens.com. 26 rooms. Breakfast room, dock, canoes. Double $130–$220 with Continental breakfast. Closed Nov.–Apr. Every room at Boothbay's **Fisherman's Wharf Inn** has a balcony with a harbor view. The inn, which is considered the "hub of the harbor," is on Pier 6, from which most sightseeing and fishing trips depart. 22 Commercial St., Boothbay Harbor, ME 04538, tel. 207/633–5090 or 800/628–6872, fax 207/633–5092, www.fishermanswharfinn.com. 54 rooms. Restaurant, bar. Double $75–$190 with Continental breakfast. Closed Nov.–mid-May. The *Argo* sails from Boothbay Harbor's Pier 6 to a Linekin Bay island for **Cabbage Island Clambake's** feasts of fish chowder, lobster, steamed clams, corn, new potatoes, and blueberry cake. Trips are conducted late June–Labor Day. Box 21, East Boothbay, ME 04544, tel. 207/633–7200. On the Sheepscot River (9G–10F), at the head of the Pemaquid Peninsula, the **Newcastle Inn** is furnished with mid-19th-century American and Asian antiques that evoke the heyday of the China Trade.

Jacuzzis and other modern luxuries are discreetly tucked away. River Rd., Newcastle, ME 04553, tel. 207/563–5685 or 800/832–8669, fax 207/563–6877, www.newcastleinn.com. 15 rooms. Restaurant, hot tubs. Double $125–$350 with full breakfast.

ABOARD THE SCHOONER *TIMBERWIND* ON MAINE'S PENOBSCOT BAY (11F–12G)
Heave Ho, Me Hearties, p. 52

The *Timberwind* is a piece of Maine maritime history. Launched in 1931, she served for decades as a pilot schooner in Portland's harbor and has never left Maine waters. Between May and October, she makes more than 30 voyages on Penobscot Bay, from which schooners traditionally hauled timber, building stone, and salt cod to ports all along the Atlantic seaboard. The 96-ft *Timberwind* is the only ship of Penobscot Bay's windjammer fleet that sails from Rockport's narrow but picturesque harbor, where schooners once picked up slaked lime from the kilns. With a captain and crew of four, she carries 20 passengers on trips of three, four, or six days. Some cruises are designated for families; others highlight lighthouses, sailing and hiking, bird-watching, folk music, or foliage. Berths fill up quickly for voyages during the full moon.

CONTACT: Schooner *Timberwind,* Box 247, Rockport, ME 04856, tel. 207/236–0801 or 800/759–9250, www.schoonertimberwind.com.

DISTANCES: Rockport (11G) is approximately halfway up the Maine coast, about 70 mi north of Portland (8H).

PRICES/HOURS: Cruises cost $349–$829 per person, with all meals. Guest sailors must provide their own wine or beer.

OPTIONS: Penobscot Bay bustled with maritime commerce in the Age of Sail, from coastal freight schooners to fully rigged ships engaged in the China Trade. "There are times when we sail out," says *Timberwind* captain Rick Miles, "that we see 15 windjammers, the way it would have been in the 1890s." The towns along the bay's west coast were famous for their sailing craft: Thomaston for its workhorse, five-masted schooners; Friendship for its graceful, inshore fishing sloops; and Searsport for its Down Easters, which were among the largest wooden sailing ships ever built. Just 27 mi north of **Rockport** on U.S. 1, tiny Searsport was a giant in 19th-century maritime trade, its shipping volume at times rivaling the ports of Boston and New York. Eleven Searsport boatyards built more than 200 deepwater ships of various rigs between 1810 and 1890, and, during the 1870s and 1880s, the village was home to a tenth of America's merchant marine captains. All this history is recounted at the **Penobscot Marine Museum.** A portrait wall shows the bearded or sideburned captains who commanded their carpenter-built vessels through 30-ft swells and 100-mph winds around Cape Horn. If they survived to see 40, most left the sea to live out their days on land in wealth and comfort. Church St., Searsport, tel. 207/548–2529, www.penobscotmarinemuseum.org. Admission: $8. Open Memorial Day weekend–Oct. 15, Mon.–Sat. 10–5 and Sun. noon–5.

A handful of stately sea captains' homes have assumed a new life as bed-and-breakfasts, including the **Homeport Inn,** built around 1861 by Captain John P. Nichols, who lived in the Victorian mansion with his family until his death in 1883. Opt for one of the larger rooms with floor-to-ceiling windows and views of the gardens, which roll down to the shore. U.S. 1, E. Main St., Searsport, ME 04974, tel. 207/548–2259 or 800/742–5814, fax 207/548–2259, www.bnbcity.com/inns/20015. 10 rooms, some share bath. Double $90 with full breakfast.

ISLE AU HAUT, DOWN EAST MAINE *(12G)*
To the Lighthouse, p. 8

French explorer Samuel de Champlain christened this bit of land Isle au Haut (High Island) in 1604, but it wasn't until 1792 that fishermen settled here. A century later they were joined by wealthy summer rusticators from Boston and New York. In 1943 about half of the 6-mi-long island was incorporated into Acadia National Park. Unlike the park's main portion on Mt. Desert Island, Isle au Haut remains rugged. Trails are infrequently cleared, and toilet facilities are limited. Trailheads lead from the island's circular, packed-dirt road to the summits of its major hills. Approximately 550 shoreline cliffs provide excellent places from which to sight seals, porpoises, and whales in the Gulf of Maine.

CONTACT: Acadia National Park, Box 177, Bar Harbor, ME 04609, tel. 207/288–3338, www.nps.gov/acad. **Isle au Haut Ferry Company,** tel. 207/367–6516, www.isleauhaut.com.

DISTANCES: Isle au Haut is accessible by a 45-minute, 6-mi mail-boat ride from Stonington (12G), which is 36 mi south of U.S. 1 via Route 15 down the Blue Hill Peninsula (12F).

PRICES/HOURS: Round-trip fare on the mail boat, which doesn't

operate on Sunday or on postal holidays, is $30. For schedules, contact the Isle au Haut Ferry Company. Admission to the Isle au Haut portion of Acadia National Park is free. Rangers are on site only mid-May through mid-Oct.

OPTIONS: The 1905 **Keeper's House Inn** has the grace of a well-built boat. The main inn's four simple bedrooms share a bath; there's also a cabin with an outhouse and an outdoor shower. Island living has a way of focusing people on essentials. Innkeepers Judi and Jeff Burke give tours of the inn's waste recycling operation and wind-powered electrical system. Electricity is used sparingly. Most illumination is by candle or lantern, and the inn has no phones or television. Meals feature local ingredients. The inn is open May 15–October, and there's a two-night minimum stay July–October 15. Box 26, Isle au Haut, ME 04645, tel. 207/367–2261 for reservations, www.keepershouse.com. 5 rooms. Double $294–$335 (plus 15% service charge) with all meals. Between May 15 and October 15, **Duck Harbor Campground**'s six lean-tos are the island's only other lodging. Requests for stays of up to three days must be made in writing after April 1 to Acadia National Park (attention Isle au Haut Reservations). Include $25 for the Special Use Permit (refunded if reservation is refused). To catch the early mail-boat ferry from Stonington, stay at the **Inn on the Harbor,** comprising four 1880s buildings and a large deck on the water. Some of its rooms have fireplaces; one room has a kitchen. Box 69, Main St., Stonington, ME 04681, tel. 207/367–2420 or 800/942–2420, fax 207/367–5165, www.innontheharbor.com. Double $105–$135 with Continental breakfast.

ROCKY COAST HIGHLIGHTS

Just before turning off Route 1 to the lobster peninsulas, stop in **Bath** (9H) to learn about the state's wooden boat-building legacy at the Maine Maritime Museum, which is in a former shipyard. North of the lobster peninsulas, **Wiscasset** (10G), "the prettiest little bottleneck in Maine," is known for its Federal architecture, good antiques shops, and fine harbor on a tidal river. In **Rockland** (11G), Penobscot Bay's largest city, the Farnsworth Art Museum specializes in art of the Maine coast, including works by Winslow Homer and the Wyeth clan. Rockland's Shore Village Museum is a must for lighthouse fans. And plan ahead for the city's Maine Lobster Festival, which takes place the first weekend in August. **Mt. Desert Island**, which contains most of Acadia National Park as well as several picturesque villages, is only an hour's drive beyond the Route 15 turnoff to Stonington–Isle au Haut from Route 1.

THE MAINE WOODS

Maine calls itself the Pine Tree State for good reason: boreal forest and spruce swamps cover about two-thirds of the state. The great northern forests begin north and west of Bangor (11E), the historic gateway to the timber camps, and stretch to Québec. Even the "highways" that traverse these northern tracts are little more than frost-heaved, two-lane, asphalt roads. You can reach many parts of the woods only by seaplane or canoe in warm months or by skis, dogsled, or snowmobile in winter. Woods roads are often private; you may have to pay a usage fee at a control gate, with the proviso that you keep your tiny auto out of the way of the dinosaur-size timber vehicles. Four-wheel drive is often an advantage and sometimes a necessity. There are actually fewer roads and inhabitants in today's wooded north country than in the 1850s, when Henry David Thoreau made his three journeys recounted in *The Maine Woods*.

QUISISANA RESORT, KEZAR LAKE, WESTERN MAINE *(7G)*

Lakeside Lyric, p. 66

Established in 1917 as a woodsy lakeside retreat for music lovers, Quisisana took on its present format (of full-service resort with musicians as housekeeping, kitchen, and dining-room staff) in the late 1940s. Occupying 47 undeveloped acres on Kezar Lake, just east of the White Mountains, Quisisana combines the leisure of summer camp with well-prepared cuisine and exceptional musical performances. Staff members are recruited from the country's leading music schools. A few one- to three-bedroom white-clapboard cottages are at the edge of pinewoods along the lake; most are a short distance back amid the trees. Small lodge rooms are available for guests on a tight budget.

CONTACT: September–June: Box 142, Larchmont, NY 10538, tel. 914/833-0293, fax 914/833-4140. June–August: Center Lovell, ME 04016, tel. 207/925-3500, www.quisisanaresort.com.

DISTANCES: Approximately 50 mi northwest of Portland (8H), via Routes 302 and 5.

PRICES/HOURS: Quisisana is open from mid-June until the fourth Saturday in August. Rates (per person, per day, double occupancy) are $115–$145 for lodge rooms and $115–$185 for cottages, including all meals, nightly entertainment, and some sports activities. A one-week minimum stay (with arrival and departure on Saturday) is expected, though shorter stays can sometimes be arranged. 11 rooms, 37 cottages. Concert hall, 3 tennis courts, windsurfing, boating, waterskiing.

OPTION: Often cited as one of the world's most beautiful lakes, 9-mi-long Kezar is surrounded by protected watershed and private camps. For the no-frills version of a week at the lake, **Gilmore Camps** rents furnished lakeside cottages built in the 1930s. The four buildings are heated with woodstoves, sleep up to five people each, have full kitchens, and enjoy the same lake views as Quisisana. Two small basic cabins without plumbing are available to house additional guests if your party is large. Contact Tom Gilmore, 23 Jorie La., Walpole, MA 02081, tel. 508/668-4489 or 800/769-3071 (or, mid-June–mid-Sept., 207/925-1933), fax 781/283-5604, www.gilmorecamps.com. $1,290–$1,690 per week per cottage; cabins (rented only in conjunction with cottages) $400 per week.

LIBBY CAMPS, LAKE MILLINOCKET, TOWNSHIP 8, RANGE 9 *(11A)*

Gone Fishing, p. 62

Starting in the 1840s, well-heeled "sports" from New York, Philadelphia, and Boston poured into the northern Maine woods by train, stagecoach, buckboard, and lake steamer to fish in elegant rusticity. They came in greater numbers after the Civil War, but the Great Depression and World War II thinned the ranks of the posh camps. The establishments that survived were those with pure intent—and really good fishing. Teddy Roosevelt spent time at Libby when the camp stood on a Lake Millinocket island; Jack Dempsey came after it was moved ashore. Unlike similar Maine establishments, Libby Camps have electricity, flush toilets, and access to 10 outposts at other wilderness lakes. They're also among the hardest camps to reach, but the reward for doing so is a wide range of waters in which to fish for brook trout, landlocked and sea-run salmon, and togue (lake trout).

CONTACT: Libby Camps, Drawer 810, Ashland, ME 04732, tel. 207/435-8274, fax 207/435-3230, www.libbycamps.com.

DISTANCES: Libby Camps are in the unorganized territory of Township 8, Range 9, about 100 air mi north of Bangor. Matt

Libby often flies guests in from Bangor, Moosehead Lake, or Lake Matagamon. To drive in, follow I-95 north from Bangor to Exit 58, then take Route 11 north to Ashland, ME (12A)–a total of about 140 mi. Libby Camps are another three-hour drive on logging roads west from Ashland.

PRICES/HOURS: Libby Camps are open for fishing from early May through September. 8 cabins. Boats, motors, canoes, tackle store (limited supplies). $130–$260 per person per day (double occupancy) with all meals.

OPTIONS: Possibly the oldest continuously operated sporting camp in the United States (since the 1850s), **Tim Pond Camps** in Eustis (8D), near the Québec border, is famed for its large brook trout and for frequent sightings of deer, moose, and bear. Box 22, Eustis, ME 04936, tel. 207/243–2947 (camp), 207/897–4056 (winter), www.timpondcamps.com. 11 cabins with hot and cold running water. Boats, canoes. $120 per person per day (double occupancy) with all meals. **Nugent's Chamberlain Lake Camps** is on the Allagash Wilderness Waterway (10A), which means that the camp must remain primitive (no running water or electricity). Primary game fish are lake trout and landlocked salmon. HCR 76, Box 632, Greenville, ME 04441, tel. 207/944–5991, www.nugentmcnallycamps.com. Accommodations range from bunks in large cabins to individual housekeeping cabins. Cabins $27.50 per person per night; bunks $45 with dinner, $80 with all meals.

DOGSLEDDING AT MOOSEHEAD LAKE, MAINE (9B–10C)
Going to the Dogs, p. 44

Moosehead Lake covers 117 square mi in northwest Maine. Greenville (10C), at the lake's southeast corner, serves as the gateway to some of the state's most rugged wilderness. The Moosehead region is famed for its fishing and hunting, but moose-spotting is fast becoming the main sport. Snowmobiles serve as both practical transportation and winter motor sport, but a few dog-mushers offer a more adventurous jaunt through the snow-covered woods.

CONTACT: Moose Country Safaris and Dogsled Trips, 191 N. Dexter Rd., Sangerville, ME 04479, tel. 207/876–4907, www.moosecountrysafaris.com.

DISTANCES: Greenville is 154 mi north of Portland via I-95 to Exit 39 (Newport). Follow signs for Route 7/11 north to Dexter (10D). In Dexter turn left onto Route 23 north. At Guilford (10D),

turn right onto Routes 6/15 to Greenville.

PRICES/HOURS: Dogsledding trips in two-person toboggan sleds are available November through March, with pickup at your lodging. One hour costs $70 per couple. Each additional hour is $30 per couple. The prices include hot food and drinks and warm sled bags. Participants should dress in layers and wear snow boots, wool socks, mittens, and a wool hat.

OPTIONS: Moosehead Lake is one of Maine's leading ice-fishing venues from December through March. Licenses and gear are available at bait shops along all the major roads. If Teddy Roosevelt and Ralph Lauren had collaborated on an inn overlooking the biggest lake in Maine's north woods, the result might have been the **Lodge at Moosehead Lake** (10C). Among the most striking features are beds into which rustic motifs—moose heads, black bears, loons, trout—have been hand-carved. Beds in the suites are suspended on massive, 19th-century, log-boom chains. All rooms have fireplaces. Lily Bay Rd., Box 1167, Greenville, ME 04441, tel. 207/695–4400, fax 207/695–2281, www.lodgeatmooseheadlake.com. 8 rooms, 3 suites. Restaurant (for guests only; open for dinner Sat. Jan.–March, Sun. and Wed. June–Oct.) Double $165–$425 with full breakfast. The **Blair Hill Inn** offers lake views and high-Victorian decor. Some guest rooms have fireplaces. Lily Bay Rd., Box 1288, Greenville, ME 04441, tel. 207/695–0224, fax 207/695–4324, www.blairhill.com. 8 rooms. Restaurant (open weekends June–Oct.; Sat. in winter for inn guests only). Double $195–$295 with full breakfast.

MAINE WOODS HIGHLIGHTS

As the northern terminus of the Appalachian Trail, the 5,267-ft plateau summit of **Mt. Katahdin** (11B) is the Holy Grail for hikers. It rises at just about the geographic center of Maine, and is the highest spot among the 46 peaks and ridges of surrounding **Baxter State Park** (11A–B). Beginning just north of the park, the 92-mi ribbon of lakes, ponds, rivers, and streams that make up the **Allagash Wilderness Waterway** (10–11A) are among North America's finest canoeing waters. If your taste runs more to the adrenaline of whitewater rafting, **the Forks** (9D), southwest of Greenville, is the best launch point onto the Kennebec River. **Greenville** itself is the prime center for moose-watching safaris in spring, summer, and early fall. The town capitalizes on its moose (over-) population with MooseMania activities from mid-May to mid-June.

Authors Patricia Harris **and** David Lyon **proudly count** themselves as New Englanders. David grew up on Maine's Penobscot Bay, where he fished for lobster in the summer, escaped to the woods the rest of the year, and took speech therapy at the university to tame his accent. Patricia hails from Connecticut, but David doesn't hold it against her, because she's the smart one. They've journeyed the world together for two decades, writing for American, British, Swiss, and Hong Kong publishers on subjects as diverse as the gypsy caves of Granada, the street markets of Shanghai, and elk migrations in the Canadian Rockies. But wherever they go, they find that it's impossible to improve on northern New England's brilliant foliage, sweet lobster, and droll Yankee wit.

Peter Guttman **is an award-winning photographer, author, lecturer, and television personality.** Creator of Fodor's *To Imagine* series, his work garnered him the 2000 Lowell Thomas Travel Journalist of the Year award. When not cruising America's backroads in his aging Saturn, he has explored every continent on assignment, journeying through more than 170 countries. His work has been published in *Condé Nast Traveler, Geo, Life, National Geographic Adventure, Outside,* and *Vogue,* and his scores of radio and television appearances include NBC's *Today,* CBS's *This Morning,* CNN, and A&E's *Top Ten.* His cyberspace kingdom is at www.peterguttman.com.